PR

PR

Fifty Years in the Field

Jack Donoghue, APR

Dundurn Press
Toronto & Oxford
1993

Edited by John Shoesmith
Printed and bound in Canada by Gagné Printing Ltd., Louiseville, Quebec

The writing of this manuscript and the publication of this book were made possible by support from several sources. The publisher wishes to acknowledge the generous assistance and ongoing support of **The Canada Council, The Book Publishing Industry Development Program** of the **Department of Communications, The Ontario Arts Council,** and **The Ontario Publishing Centre** of the **Ministry of Culture, Tourism and Recreation.**

Care has been taken to trace the ownership of copyright material used in the text (including the illustrations). The author and publisher welcome any information enabling them to rectify any reference or credit in subsequent editions.

J. Kirk Howard, Publisher

Canadian Cataloguing in Publication Data

Donoghue, Jack, 1916–
      PR : fifty years in the field

ISBN 1-55002-164-8

1. Donoghue, Jack, 1916– . 2. Public relations – Canada – Biography. I. Title.

FC601.D65A3 1993   659.2'092   C92-095296-8
F1034.3.D65A3 1993

Dundurn Press Limited	Dundurn Distribution	Dundurn Press Limited
2181 Queen Street East	73 Lime Walk	1823 Maryland Avenue
Suite 301	Headington, Oxford	P.O. Box 1000
Toronto, Canada	England	Niagara Falls, N.Y.
M4E 1E5	0X3 7AD	U.S.A., 14302-1000

CONTENTS

Foreword   ix
Preface   xi
Acknowledgements   xii

PART ONE: The Military

Chapter One: History   3

Personal history. The Great Depression. Education. Banff Springs Golf Course. Royalty. Journalism. The Second World War. PR in the field. The Maple Leaf. *Repatriation.*

Chapter Two: Exercise Muskox   14

A ground force of 47 soldiers and scientists in 12 snowmobiles makes a 3,100-mile trek through the Arctic, from Fort Churchill, Manitoba, to Edmonton, Alberta. Their objective is "to prove men and machines against northern conditions and to gather scientific data." The PR objective is to get the story told so that the Canadian public is made aware of a role their armed forces can play in peacetime.

Chapter Three: The Hong Kong Courts Martial   26

The horrors of the battle for Hong Kong and the subsequent atrocities result in the post-war courts martial of one Canadian and two British non-commissioned officers. The military trials present special PR problems. This chapter deals with how these are met.

Chapter Four: Redramp   35

Manitoba's 1950 flood provides valuable PR experience. Two Canadian officers attend a U.S. Armed Forces PR school. Winnipeg faces complete inundation. This chapter documents the PR actions and results, the crisis in army-government relations, and plans for the city's evacuation.

Chapter Five: Manitoba's 1953 Polio Epidemic   52

Canada's last major polio epidemic becomes highly personal when the author's daughter is afflicted with the disease and he is requested to solve the epidemic's major PR problem.

Chapter Six: Germany   62

Six thousand Canadian soldiers, serving in a foreign land in peacetime, accompanied by their wives and children, offer an ideal situation for acquiring knowledge of community relations and other facets of the PR function.

Chapter Seven: Nigeria   76

A former director of public relations (army) applies what he has learned about PR to the resolution of charges of genocide in the Nigerian Civil War of 1967–70.

Chapter Eight: PR and Royalty   86

The author plans for royal visits while in the army and in the public sector.

PART TWO: The Public Sector

Chapter Nine: Information Canada   99

Early history of PR in Canada's public sector. Post-war PR in the federal government. Creation and demise of Information Canada.

Chapter Ten: Farewell to Arms – Now, the Public Service   108

The author joins the federal public service Department of Manpower and Immigration. His first task is to learn and execute the PR aspects of launching a federal White Paper. A transfer to the Department of Energy, Mines and Resources. A new approach to presenting proposed federal legislation. PR and the Canada Water Act.

Chapter Eleven: Hudson 70   119

> *The flagship of Canada's scientific fleet, css Hudson,*
> *circumnavigates South and North America. This voyage changes the*
> *thinking about the method of transporting oil from the Arctic. An*
> *examination of the PR problems involved.*

PART THREE: The Private Sector

Chapter Twelve: A Park for All Seasons   133

> *Calgary's citizens, with the help of a PR plan, participate in designing*
> *a park for all seasons.*

Chapter Thirteen: Alberta Nurses' Strike, 1977   143

> *The role of PR in this historic strike.*

Chapter Fourteen: Canmore Mines   150

> *A mine that operated in Canmore, Alberta, for 89 years closes with*
> *no criticism from labour, management, or government. The role PR*
> *played.*

Chapter Fifteen: Public Relations and
              the Abuse of Political Power   156

> *The fight waged by the Independent Petroleum Association of*
> *Canada against the National Energy Program.*

Chapter Sixteen: A Look Beneath the Bottom Line   166

> *"The public relations profession has a crucial role to play in the new*
> *order of things that will confront society in the '90s" – a past*
> *president of the Canadian Public Relations Society identifies the*
> *problems and provides guidance for business, industry, government*
> *and PR practitioners.*

Chapter Seventeen: Reflections   175

A comparison of PR in the military, public, and private sectors. PR people in the early days. PR education. Contributions of the professional organizations: CPRS and IABC. Dramatic changes in the CPRS and IABC. Women in PR. Federal bilingual policy. Access to government information. Practising in the military, the public sector, and the private sector. The importance of direct access for the head of PR to the head of an organization. The necessity for the head of PR to be a full member of the organization's management committee. The PR agency. Technology. Television. The future. Ethics.

FOREWORD

Jack and I were born in the same 24-hour period, 33 years apart. We are both Aquarians.

It has been said that those who are born under this fixed air sign will labour with love if they select a profession that is always changing and which involves the intellect. Labour with love we do.

We are both now senior public relations consultants in Calgary, Jack in semi-retirement and I at mid-career. This book is partly about the evolution of our profession and partly about Jack's evolution as a professional.

As one in the public relations profession, I read this book straight through, cover to cover. But you can also read a chapter here and a chapter there, somewhat like a book of short stories. Each chapter can stand alone.

You can read as one interested in vignettes from our recent past about some events that have not been given much space in Canadian history books. You can read as one outside the public relations profession looking in at some examples of the kinds of things we really do. I'd venture that many a PR student will be reading certain chapters at certain points in their studies, and be given assignments from teachers in search of Canadian content. This is a book that can be read any way you want, and from many different points of view.

Jack's conversational style makes the reading a pleasure, but within each chapter, or case, he draws out some useful lessons in PR.

Everyone should have a mentor to give perspective, to give advice when asked, and to give encouragement, whether it is solicited or not. Jack is my mentor. With this book, and as one of the deans of public relations in Canada, he is mentoring many more than just myself.

The author caught me at a very good time: in mid-career. Some books are especially relevant when you've been doing something for 20 years and have another 20 more to go. This is one of them.

At mid-career, Jack was still practising his profession in the army. Ahead of him lay a career in the public service and a career in the private sector. Between the lines, one lesson for me in Jack's book is that this profession truly does have many fields in which it can be practised and offers many challenges through which to stretch and grow intellectually. And the second lesson to be drawn about the profession is that it, too, is stretching and growing, because of the people who practise it.

Public relations is still a labour of love for Jack. This is one of the ways he expresses that love.

Thanks Jack.

Judi Gunter, APR

PREFACE

This book has three parts that follow the sequence in which I spent my life in the practice of PR.

I.   PR in the military
II.   PR in the public sector
III.   PR in the private sector

Each part is comprised of a series of chapters relating experiences in solving public relations problems, the solutions which ensued, and the lessons learned.

I hope the description of these experiences will prove helpful to corporate and government executives, PR practitioners, and PR students seeking to expand their knowledge of PR, or any one of its pseudonyms – "communications," "government relations," "investor relations," or "public affairs."

Whether used as an instructional or informational tool, this book now provides a body of knowledge, dedicated solely to Canadian accomplishments, taking its place beside the formidable American collections on our nation's bookshelves.

ACKNOWLEDGEMENTS

Douglas Shenstone, of Ottawa, edited my first book and the first draft of this book before his death in 1991. He was a master craftsman of words, and a veteran who survived the 1942 tragedy of Dieppe.

A special thanks is due to John Shoesmith who edited subsequent drafts and provided helpful guidance, as did Judith Turnbull – both of Dundurn Press.

John Francis gave me the opportunity to try my wings in the private sector and provided wise counsel as I made the transition from the public sector. His chapter, "A Look Below the Bottom Line," contains observations useful to corporate executives and students alike.

Judi Gunter's foreword pinpoints some of my strongly held beliefs. The profession, indeed, "has many fields in which it can be practised." If I succeed in expanding the knowledge of readers about "the kinds of things we *really* do," the effort to write this book will have been worth it.

Thanks are also due to Trish Jordan who produced the manuscript of this book as well as my earlier book, *The Edge of War,* published in 1988. She displayed great patience and made important format suggestions. She was assisted by Terrie Regier.

Finally, I am deeply grateful to St. Jude, who frequently has found solutions for many of my problems.

PART ONE

THE MILITARY

CHAPTER 1

HISTORY

A golf course, a boyhood chum, the Great Depression, and a war diverted me from the medical profession and drew me into a life-long career in public relations, practised today under a number of different titles, including "public affairs." (These days it seems many affairs are made public.)

Because my mother wanted to be with her sister, her only living relative, I was born in Kingston, Ontario, on 1 February, 1916, the home of my parents before their marriage. Shortly after my arrival, mother returned to my father in Winnipeg with my sister, Doretta, and her new son.

My first grade of elementary education was taken in Kingston when, following a brief summer vacation, my uncle and aunt successfully pleaded with me parents to let me remain with them for my first year of school. Jack and "Minn" Doherty had no children.

The remainder of my elementary education was taken in Winnipeg and St. Mary's, followed by attendance at St. Paul's High School and then St. Paul's College, an affiliate of the University of Manitoba. Both institutions are run by the Jesuit Order.

I began to lean towards the medical profession as a result of a chum, Jim MacLean, the son of the University of Manitoba's president. Although we didn't go to the same schools, we did hang around together. Jim was a little older and had two older brothers, one who became a journalist, the other, a doctor. The latter, Alec, did well in medicine and, ultimately, became the senior diagnostician at the Mayo Clinic in Rochester, New York. He was also an outstanding swimmer. Jim kept me informed about Alec's progress and he became something of a hero for me.

But a medical career for me was not to be. The Great Depression got in the way. Neither my family nor I could have generated sufficient funds for such an expensive education, and I wasn't scholarship material. I never raised the subject of medical school with my family. But with the help of my father, I was able to attend St. Paul's College and obtain a degree.

Dad was chief clerk in the paymaster's office of the Canadian Pacific Railway. When I was on the verge of completing high school, he had me make a formal application for employment as a caddy at the golf course of the CPR hotel in Banff, Alberta. I was fortunate to get the job, and for that first summer after high school I lived in staff quarters at the Banff Springs Hotel, working for the golf professional, Tim Thomson, an elderly Scot who had been taught by the legendary Harry Varden. In his prime, Tim was considered one of the greatest exponents of the 5-iron. (I believe in those days it was called a mashie.)

I was appointed caddy master during my second year at Banff Springs, which provided me with an initial experience in management. I made enough money each summer to contribute to my upkeep and education. Dad took care of any shortfall.

When I returned to Winnipeg in the fall after my first summer at Banff Springs, I went to see Jim, who had begun working for British United Press (BUP). I told him about the dignitaries and Hollywood stars I'd seen at the Banff Springs, for some of whom I had caddied. Almost instantly, Jim recruited me as a "stringer" for the next three seasons. I sent him brief news stories and was paid for those that were used. I dispatched articles on such personalities as Hollywood stars Ginger Rogers, Kate Smith, and Bing Crosby; the King of Siam; the postmaster general of the United States, "Big" Jim Farley; and industrialist R.J. Reynolds, who owned the tobacco company that produced Camel cigarettes. It was a great place for stories.

I was jobless when I graduated from St. Paul's College in the spring of 1939. The CPR requested that I serve as a lifeguard at the hotel's two swimming pools during the Royal Visit of King George VI and the Queen (presently, the popular Queen "Mum"), scheduled to take place before the hotel would open to the public. I accepted immediately. When I told Jim, he made arrangements for the BUP correspondent covering the visit to call upon me if he needed help. I met him, but he didn't need my assistance.

One afternoon, dressed in my white T-shirt, slacks, and running shoes, I was standing on the walkway that separated the outdoor pool from the indoor pool. There were no swimmers in either one. The roof of the indoor pool formed part of the large patio facing the spectacular Bow Valley view. A low wall extended across the outside of the ceiling of the indoor pool, about 20 feet above my head.

I heard a commotion and several voices on the patio. I stepped out from the wall to the edge, turned around and looked up. Looking over the wall and directly at me were the King and Queen and Prime Minister Mackenzie King. I froze for several seconds, not knowing whether to salute, bow formally from the waist, or genuflect. The Queen then smiled. I smiled back and quickly walked into the indoor pool area. As it turned out, this was not to be my first brush with royalty.

At season's end I went to Vancouver to visit Jim and to ask for a job. "Hang your coat over there," he said, pointing to a hatrack. "There's a desk and a typewriter. You're hired." This indicated a future in journalism and, though I didn't realize it, the beginning of my career.

The Second World War broke out in the fall, but I didn't rush to enlist. Having experienced the Depression, I was more afraid of unemployment than the war. Of course, I knew nothing about war. What I did know was that I wanted more journalism experience before considering enlisting. The Vancouver Bureau of BUP provided that experience. The staff was small, enabling me to cover a wide variety of subjects and events, such as politics, sports, business, and science.

The first major story I covered that received continent-wide attention was one I didn't write. It was titled "Diary of Death." The bureau received a tip that two trappers had slowly starved to death on Vancouver Island and that they had kept a daily diary. They had moved into their cabin in the spring and, hence, didn't know the war had started. Game on the island that year was scarce and fishing was poor. They became too weak to walk out of the cabin. The pilot of a seaplane based on Zeballos, on the northwest coast of the island, dropped in to visit them and found the dead bodies and the diary.

The only communication from Vancouver to Zeballos was B.C. radio telephone and prolonged static frustrated the attempt of Vancouver news organizations to complete a call. By a stroke of luck, I got through to the Zeballos operator just as the static ceased; as long as I held the airwaves, no one else could get through.

The operator confirmed the scant details we had and when I enquired about the diary, she said, "Oh, I have it here."

I asked her to read a few entries, then skip a few, and read again. The diary was written tightly, in simple but dramatic and emotional sentences. I asked her to return to the beginning and start reading it again while I typed what she read. It resulted in the longest B.C. radio telephone call up to that time, about three hours.

As I finished typing each few pages, Alex Janusitis, the bureau manager who had replaced Jim when he left to cover the Aleutian Islands landing (launched for fear of a Japanese attack), tore off the paper in the typewriter. After writing a lead to the story, he put it on the news wire with a copyright. Enthusiastic reaction from United Press, New York, and BUP Montreal was instantaneous. They wanted more.

While I was transcribing, Janusitis arranged for Ron Dodds, a member of staff, to fly to Zeballos, where he convinced the pilot to allow him to board the plane and fly to the cabin to bring back the bodies. Dodds not only got the closing story of the saga, he also obtained interior and exterior photos of the cabin. In newspaper terms, it was a "clean beat."

The closing sentence of the diary couldn't have been written better by a skilled professional. It read: "Jim died today."

After writing it, the young trapper shot himself.

I was also sent to Edmonton to cover Alberta Premier William Aberhart's last election in 1940. I stayed in a hotel popular with ranchers and farmers to gauge their opinion about the election. As well, I buttonholed store clerks and blue-collar workers to learn about their feelings towards the Social Credit party.

Aberhart's fiscal policies of "funny money" were laughed at, but he had given them honest government. Under Aberhart, citizens who worked overtime had to be adequately compensated, by law; mobile dental clinics had been established to serve residents of the rural areas; and the public school system had undergone significant improvement.

The Conservatives and Liberals joined forces for the election, with a member of only one of the two parties running against a Socred candidate. Nearly every advance story written predicted a Social Credit defeat. Because of my discussions with ranchers, farmers, blue-collar workers, and clerks, my advance story disagreed. I forecast that Aberhart would be returned to office with the loss of but a few seats. To my satisfaction, that is just what happened.

I was learning something about popular opinion and journalism. I was also learning how reporters worked, how they approached news, and why they did the things they did, knowledge that was fundamental for a PR individual and that would serve me well in the years to come. After the war, when the function of public relations rapidly expanded, journalists were the main segment of the population from which PR people were drawn.

Not long after the election, I was transferred to the Winnipeg Bureau. I took a holiday to visit a classmate in Guelph who had joined the Jesuit Order. I then moved on to Montreal to visit my father's youngest brother, Joe, and his wife, Floss. They arranged a blind date with a member of the Clancy family, Colleen. We had a marvellous evening touring the city's nightspots and a year later, in 1941, when Colleen visited a close friend and former schoolmate in Winnipeg, we became engaged. We were married the following year on 6 June 1942 in Montreal, a date that was to become very significant two years later.

By that time, conscription had been passed by Parliament. I had gained the experience I felt I needed and I didn't want to be dragged kicking and screaming into the army. Colleen and I agreed: I would enlist after the wedding. It was a wonderful 51-day honeymoon!

Before enlisting, I'd never met a PR person or seen a news release. When I was processed at Military District (MD) No. 10's Recruiting Depot, the army learned all about me, including the fact that I had worked for a wire service. I was told that within a few days I would be sent to the Infantry Basic Training Centre, located on the University of Manitoba campus. In the meantime, I was to report to the MD No. 10 headquarters' public relations office in Fort Osborne Barracks. There I observed an operation similar to that of a weekly newspaper. News releases about members of the army were being written and sent mostly to the smaller rural newspapers. In the few days that I was there, reporters seeking information came to the office and were provided with it, or appropriate interviews were arranged. It was my first glimpse of PR.

I learned nothing about PR operations overseas until basic training. Two weeks before the two-month course ended, a messenger came to the training area with orders for me to report to the adjutant. On arrival – and after I saluted – the adjutant invited me to sit down. He told me journalists were being sought to serve in army public relations. They would attain the rank of senior non-commissioned officer and be assigned overseas to a fighting unit of the infantry, armoured corps, or artillery. There they would facilitate war correspondents (Warcos) who came to their unit. In the absence of a Warco, the non-commissioned PR officer would write the story of the unit's actions and, through the PR organization, it would be passed to the media. He asked if I was interested. That should have surprised me but, being a new recruit, I wasn't yet aware that privates were generally *told* what they were going to do, not *asked*.

It didn't take me long to realize that I'd be retaining and expanding some of the journalism skills I had learned and, thus, would make it less difficult for me to obtain employment when the war ended. I said I was interested and that I had spent a few days in the MD No. 10 headquarters' PR office before arriving at the training centre. I didn't know it, but I had just left my journalism career and moved into a lifetime career of public relations that would see me practise in the military, the public and private sectors.

The army proved to be an excellent place to start, even though it didn't turn out the way the adjutant had described. Few people realized, including myself, that the military had been in the PR business for a long, long time.

American Ivy Lee is often considered to be the founding father of public relations. Historically, however, many army generals were centuries ahead of him – Caesar and Bonaparte, to name just two. Caesar kept a flow of letters moving by messengers from the Gallic war zones to home. Bonaparte was quoted as saying he "feared a hostile press more than two enemy divisions." It is not inconceivable that both generals asked their returning messengers, "What are the boys saying now?"

In the Great War of 1914–18, Canadian newspapers published accounts provided by British war correspondents. No Canadian Army public relations organization existed.

From 1918 to 1939, the Canadian Army made little use of PR (then called press relations); when they did it was usually only defensively. Press officers were not trained in media relations and their press responsibilities were in addition to their regimental duties. The outbreak of the Second World War changed all that.

The Department of National Defence and its armed forces mishandled the public relations function in the early days of the war. One lone army major, a veteran of the First World War, was appointed chief press liaison officer for the entire department. Everyone gave interviews, so factual information became garbled.

Prominent journalists, including Dave Rogers, Grant Dexter, R.S. (Dick) Malone (later to head army public relations in the field overseas), and Charles Vinning (a friend of Prime Minister Mackenzie King), carried out specific assignments for Defence Minister J.L. Ralston. Frequently, however, the government did not listen. For example, when the first German prisoner of war escaped from a camp, the Cabinet decided not to inform the press and the public. The prisoner successfully crossed the St. Lawrence to the United States. The press there broke the story and the resulting criticism nearly brought about the Canadian government's downfall.

Ralston persuaded Dick Malone to coordinate the public relations function for the armed forces. Malone travelled from coast to coast setting up public relations services for the army, navy, and air force in each district. Joseph Clark was appointed head of all three services, reporting to the defence minister. The PR services under Clark were charged with the responsibility of providing: a) information to the people of Canada; b) information from overseas (from war correspondents) to the people of Canada; c) information to Canadian troops through the daily military newspaper, *The Maple Leaf*; and d) weighted information to the enemy through the Psychological Warfare Branch.

From 1942 until the war's end, the armed forces' public relations services underwent refinements and expansion that could not have been imagined in 1939. Each service learned to work with not only Canadian war correspondents, but with those from Allied nations. Although correspondents covered all three services, the weight of coverage was directed towards the army because of the nature of army operations.

News editors were reluctant to assign reporters to convoys for the long voyage to and from Britain. (In the Persian Gulf War in 1991, the Canadian Navy did not overlook the opportunities presented by the geography of the Middle East and had berths available for war correspondents, who could travel to and from the Canadian warships.) Coverage of the air force was carried out by briefings for war correspondents and air crew interviews.

Overseas, army public relations groups were placed in the field in Italy and northwest Europe with the objective of serving war correspondents who provided information to the people at home and to the Allies. Through these groups, war correspondents were provided with clothing, meals, accommodation, transportation, censorship, and transmission facilities.

Each PR group was composed of:

- A conducting section to transport Warcos.
- Combat photographers and cameramen.
- *The Maple Leaf* publishing section.
- A communications section to transmit copy and film.
- A censorship section.
- A Psychological Warfare section.
- An administration section.

Canadian war correspondents had their stories out first on the invasions of Sicily, Italy, and Normandy, and the liberations of Rome and Paris. Army cameramen's films of the invasion of Normandy were the first on the newsreels of the day, showing Canadian soldiers overrunning the beach.

The movement of copy and film from Normandy to the Ministry of Information in London, England, had been well planned in advance. Colonel Eric Gibbs who became head of *Time* and *Life* magazines for Europe following the war was the key Canadian in planning message centres for the Ministry of Information, located at the University of London. Supreme Headquarters Allied Expeditionary Forces' plan provided for the movement of copy during the invasion and until the troops in France were firmly entrenched with effective communications equipment on the continent.

Shortly after arriving overseas, I was assigned to General Eisenhower's Supreme Headquarters Allied Expeditionary Force (SHAEF) to participate in planning the method by which Warcos' copy, film, and recordings for broadcast would be transmitted from "far shore" (Normandy) to "near shore" (Britain). The plan provided for wireless transmission of the stories from the Normandy beaches. Film and wire recordings were placed in a canvas bag lettered P-R-E-S-S. Stories could also be placed in the bag. The bag was thrown to sailors whose vessels were about to leave the beaches for the return trip to Britain. Attached was a tag instructing the sailors to get the bag to soldiers wearing red and white PRESS armbands on the docks of the British port they entered. The soldiers then notified the PR message centre, which arranged for pickup of the bag. Light aircraft, dispatch riders, and teletype equipment were used to get the stories and film to the Ministry of Information in London.

Malone linked a high-speed Creed teletype to the army's No. 33 field set. This enabled Canadian PR to clear thousands of words from the beaches the first day of the invasion. It also resulted in the Canadian Warco stories reaching Britain first.

Message centres had been established in Southampton, Portsmouth, and Plymouth about two weeks before 6 June 1944. I was posted to the Southampton Centre and in early August, I joined No. 3 PR Group, then at Rots in Normandy. Rots is close to Carpiquet where Canadian troops had fought a bloody battle on the Carpiquet airport.

For the next five months, I conducted Warcos to formations and units at the front. My driver and I would take two correspondents in a jeep to units they had informed me the previous evening that they wished to visit.

My first trip was with Ross Munro. I had known Munro before either of us had joined the army. He worked for Canadian Press in Winnipeg. When the war ended, Ross had covered every major battle in which the Canadian Army had participated in Italy and northwest Europe.

Subsequently, I conducted Charles Lynch of Reuters, Ralph Allen of *Maclean's* magazine, Lionel Shapiro of the North American Newspaper Alliance and *Maclean's*, and Alan Randall of Canadian Press. We covered the final clearing of Caen, the drive to close the Falaise Gap and the annihilation of the German 7th Army, the Canadian entry into Dieppe, the clearing of the channel ports, Boulogne and Calais, and the assault landings at Breskens and Flushing. The last correspondents I conducted were Ben Malkin of the *Winnipeg Free Press* and Bill Bonni, an American Warco working for Associated Press who had served previously in the Pacific Theatre.

Following two spells of illness, Malone sent me to Brussels to join *The Maple Leaf* as adjutant and I was later appointed assistant editor. I remained with the newspaper until I was repatriated to Canada in June 1945.

I learned a great deal from Malone, a pre-war journalist who gained his military experience with the miltia before the war. After the war, he became one of the most prominent figures in Canadian journalism, first as publisher of the *Winnipeg Free Press* and later the *Globe and Mail.*

Malone based operations of the PR units on a series of principles. While serving in northwest Europe, I knew our work was effective and I identified some of the principles – though I didn't think of them as being principles. I hadn't enough experience to recognize that many functions of planning and management adhered to principles. After I gained further experience, I was able to identify these principles by which we had worked.

1. Warcos were vital members of the armed forces, and the armed forces were dependent on the Canadian public.
2. The PR planning was an integral part of army operational planning.
3. Malone had direct access to both the Commander of 1st Canadian Army and the director of PR at National Defence, Ottawa, as well as his PR units. Thus, he could express directly to the head of 1st Canadian Army, the head of PR at National Defence and his units the policies and programs that would contribute to operations.
4. Warcos had the right to report what they learned and saw, subject only to the maintenance of security. Only information valuable to the enemy was to be deleted from their dispatches.

5. Formal and informal operational briefings and impromptu interviews were provided to the Warcos by senior operations officers at all field formations and units.
6. Army PR provided Warcos with transport, conducting officers, drivers, rations, and accommodation.
7. Rapid transmission of stories, film, and recordings to Canada was an army PR responsibility.
8. Army censors must understand that only information helpful to the enemy is censorable. Trained military censors who have been employed in media relations and understand the media make the best censors – not regimental officers.
9. Warcos were free to move anywhere in the battle zone, if accompanied by a conducting officer.
10. The competitive character of journalism was respected. Competing journalists were not to travel in the same jeep. On returning from the front to the PR unit, conducting officers were forbidden to discuss with others what they had seen, learned, or heard.
11. Where facilities were in short supply, or access limited, priority was given to wire services (e.g., Canadian Press), broadcasting networks, and individual publications with large circulations.

These policies paid dividends. In 1938, Ross Munro wrote the foreword to my first book, *The Edge of War*, in which he said:

> In the Second World War, the Canadian government and the three services recognized it was vital that the armed forces overseas had the support of the Canadian public, particularly with the volunteer system of enlistment.
>
> So, from a meagre beginning, public relations organizations were developed within the services to facilitate coverage of the war correspondents and broadcasters in the Mediterranean and northwest Europe. These reporters were the credible link between the men at the front and the people at home. The Canadian Public Relations (PR) units became highly efficient, recognized as probably the best and most cooperative in the Allied forces.

During the war, Warcos of other countries wrote stories about Canadian Army PR that expressed the same opinion.

The Maple Leaf assignment resulted in mixed emotions. I missed the excitement of the battle zone, but I had returned to newspaper work. This, I thought, would help me sharpen my skills for the return to civilian life and help me to get employment after the war. The adjutant's responsibilities also taught me aspects of administration.

Occasionally, Malone gave me features to write, but he denied my request to return to conducting. I had moved to the newspaper shortly before Christmas 1944.

In May 1945, I was repatriated to MD No. 10. The General Officer Commanding (GOC) had lost the public relations officer at Fort Osborne to civilian life. He had refused to accept a replacement unless the replacement was an officer with overseas PR experience. Captain Jack Golding, a fellow officer writing for *The Maple Leaf,* was scheduled to fill the position because he wanted to be with his father in Canada, who was seriously ill. However, before the move could be made, Jack's father died. He told Malone that he no longer wished to return to Canada. Without informing me, Jack recommended that I should fill the position.

When Malone told me of the transfer, I pointed out that there were no compassionate grounds for the move. He replied that I was being posted because I had overseas experience in the field and had previously served in MD No. 10. The matter was settled.

I arrived home in June 1945, a little more than a year after I had left.

CHAPTER 2

EXERCISE MUSKOX

Exercise Muskox radically changed my career plans. Shortly after I reported to headquarters, I was introduced to the General Officer Commanding, Brigadier R.O.G. Morton. Officer selection for the peacetime army had begun when Morton asked me if I would consider joining. I explained that my intention was to return to journalism. He didn't press the point, but informed me that the army would soon launch its first major peacetime exercise and he believed it was vital that the Canadian public be informed about the event. He recognized that public understanding of the army's role would influence its future and the future of its units.

He believed that the many PR lessons learned during the war should be carried over into peacetime – one of these being effective public relations.

Morton had seen the easy access Warcos had to briefing officers at all levels in the battle zone. He also had seen the trust that had developed between the army and the Warcos. He wanted to maintain that trust in peacetime.

The military exercise about which Morton expressed concern was eventually named "Muskox," a trek of about 3,100 miles across the Arctic from Churchill, Manitoba, to Edmonton, Alberta.

Morton hoped that British United Press (BUP) would permit me to remain with him, assuming my release would be granted before the exercise was completed. I told him I was planning to meet my civilian manager, R.W. (Bob) Keyserlingk, and obtain his views when I visited Montreal.

In Montreal, I met Keyserlingk and he told me that when I returned to BUP, I would face a decision as to whether to remain with the news agency or move to a new position. He was not prepared to provide me with the details until I had been released from the army. I told him about the brigadier's wishes and explained that, because the army had been good to me, I would like to do what Morton was requesting. Keyserlingk agreed.

I was pleased with the decision and when I returned to Winnipeg, I told the brigadier that I would be able to remain until the conclusion of Exercise Muskox. I estimated my release would not come before that date – around April/May 1946.

However, three days after my return to Winnipeg, a letter from Keyserlingk propelled Colleen and me into a state of turmoil. The letter said that if I remained in the army until the conclusion of the exercise, I must release BUP from its legal obligation to rehire me. The "first in, first out" policy was reinforced by legislation that obligated an employer to rehire an employee released from the armed forces. This had not been discussed during the meeting in Montreal. As my anger rose, I gathered my pride. No company need rehire me because of a "legal obligation," and so I wrote Keyserlingk.

When I informed the brigadier, he repeated his suggestion that I apply for a peacetime commission and, with Colleen's agreement, I did.

I pushed my letter of resignation to BUP halfway into the post box and said to Colleen, "Do you still agree?"

"Yes," she replied, "if this is what you want."

With that, I tipped the letter into the box. It was a decision I have never regretted.

After a series of tests and an interview with a panel of officers, I was granted a commission in the army in 1945.

Exercise Muskox was my first large peacetime PR project. The name was chosen because of the shoulder-to-shoulder circular defence formation adopted by the shaggy beasts of the North when threatened. While the operational objective was "to prove men and machines against northern conditions and to gather scientific data," the public relations objective was to inform Canadians of an important peacetime army and air force role.

The start line of the exercise was Fort Churchill, a military base 600 miles north of Winnipeg. Like the federal government's policy towards the north, Churchill's history as a civilian port and a military base followed an up-and-down course.

Jens Munck, originally from Denmark, camped with his party in the area during the winter of 1619–20. He was probably the first European to settle there, but the cost was tragic. Sixty-two members of his expedition died during that winter. Only Munck and two sailors survived.

The Hudson's Bay Company began construction of a trading post at Churchill in 1689, but it was destroyed by fire before it was ever completed. Twenty-seven years later, in 1716, another post was built by James Knight.

The first military establishment was Fort Prince of Wales, which the Hudson's Bay Company constructed over a period of 38 years to defend the area from the French. Although the design of the fort represented 18th-century state of the art, its garrison of 39 men surrendered in 1782 to France's Admiral La Perouse and his 400 men.

In the fall of 1931, the fortunes of Churchill rose sharply as the railroad was opened with the objective of providing the Prairie provinces with an ocean port, primarily for the purpose of shipping grain.

During the Second World War, Fort Churchill's military importance was re-established when it provided a staging field for U.S. planes en route to Britain. Had the German-planned invasion of the United Kingdom achieved any measure of success, the same route would have been valuable for the evacuation of wounded.

When the war ended, Churchill's military component was not only retained but expanded, with the Canadian army taking over the base and creating an experimental and training centre in 1946. The centre included components of National Defence Research and the Royal Canadian Air Force.

Before Exercise Muskox, there was concern that Fort Churchill would be regarded as a secret base designed to oppose the Russians. Val Werier of the *Winnipeg Tribune*, who covered the Exercise Muskox take off from Fort Churchill and its arrival in Baker Lake, N.W.T., wrote: "The quickest way to irk the men (of Muskox) is to suggest defence research against Russia as the trip's objective. The only research weapons are small arms and pistols."

Even after Muskox, the idea of Fort Churchill being a base of military secrets persisted. As a result, I recommended that a party of print and broadcast journalists be given a tour of the base. The commandant of Fort Churchill, Lieutenant-Colonel Jim Tedlie, agreed with my suggestion and immediately implemented a plan which solved the problem.

Invitations were extended to the media and about 10 of them were accepted. Accompanied by me, the party was flown to Churchill where Tedlie and several of his officers met us. Tedlie, a Highland officer, was accustomed (especially in winter) to meeting visitors at the airport clad in his kilt — a rather breezy garment up against Churchill's winter chill. On this day, however, he wore parka trousers, over which were Bermuda-length shorts of the same material as the trousers. The hem of one leg had

Soldiers standing guard on the ramparts of Fort Prince of Wales during Exercise Muskox. It had been well over a century since such a guard had been mounted.
Courtesy National Archives of Canada, PA 171354.

an inch-long fringe. The other officers wore identical clothing, complete with the unusual fringe.

Following an official welcome and briefing, the journalists spent two days at the camp. Immediately after the initial briefing, one or two of the reporters raised questions concerning the purpose of the fringe. Each question was answered with a curt, "I'm sorry, but that's classified."

During their stay, the reporters and broadcasters were shown all the base facilities and were briefed on its military and scientific projects. Nonetheless, questions about the fringe persisted right up to the final briefing before the party's departure for Winnipeg. During the briefing, Tedlie acknowledged the interest that had been shown in the fringe and stated that its purpose had now been declassified.

Colonel Jim Tedlie (left) in his customary dress for greeting guests arriving in Churchill – a kilt, even in winter! Next to Tedlie is the Honourable Brooke Claxton and staff officers of the air force and army at Fort Churchill.
Courtesy Department of National Defence.

"The purpose of the fringe," Tedlie told them, "was to ensure that each of you, before you left Churchill, would have one leg longer than the other. We've been pulling your leg." The only secret in Churchill was the fringe.

Tedlie's plan worked. One published story began: "The only secret weapon in Fort Churchill is a fringe worn around a trouser leg." The article went on to describe the commandant's joke and the facilities and projects at the base.

Tedlie was an effective commandant. One of his innovations was the "bread and butter" lecture, whereby each scientist was required to give, upon arrival at Fort Churchill, a lecture describing his project to the military personnel. This created a rapport between the soldiers and the scientists.

Through November and December 1945, 55 gunners, craftsmen, privates, and signallers underwent training and competed for places as drivers, mechanics, and radio operators on the 12 Penguin snowmobiles to be used on Exercise Muskox. These vehicles had been designed during the war for the planned invasion of Norway. They could transport four to six occupants and tow a tractor-trailer loaded with 6,000 pounds of supplies and equipment.

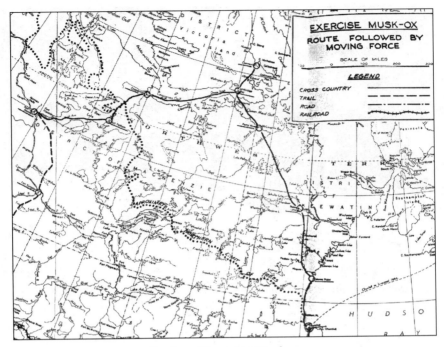

Route of Exercise Muskox.
Courtesy Department of National Defence.

Six-foot tall Colonel P.C. Baird, 34 years old and leader of the moving force, was known to his Eskimo friends as "Tatigak," their word for a "great blue heron bird."

The route of the 47 soldiers (eight positions had been dropped) and scientists in their 12 mechanical snowshoes, the Penguins, stretched from Churchill to Baker Lake, and north to Cambridge Bay on Victoria Island where the detachment crossed Denmark Bay. The force then crossed Coronation Gulf to Coppermine, then to Port Radium's Fort Norman and Fort Nelson, and finally to Edmonton.

Initially, the PR tasks were straightforward. What I had learned in northwest Europe was useful, but I was confined to the care of reporters and improving their needed facilities. Thus, I spent January 1946 preparing an information kit and extending invitations to the newspapers, wire services, and radio stations to cover the exercise when the scientists and soldiers crossed the start line at Fort Churchill.

Other administrative tasks included arranging accommodation, meals, and briefings for the reporters, done through the commandant at Fort

A Dakota aircraft is being unloaded of technical equipment and luggage at
Cambridge Bay, N.W.T., 20 March 1946.
Courtesy National Archives of Canada, PA 134304.

Churchill. Through the Royal Canadian Air Force Headquarters in
Winnipeg, I arranged for transportation. The signals officer at Fort
Osborne ensured that the newspaper reporters would be permitted to file
their stories out of the army signals office at Churchill.

The difficult problems came later.

On 15 February 1946, journalists were flown to Churchill for a 9:30
a.m. briefing and to witness the start of the expedition. Despite the blind-
ing sunshine and -43°F weather, coverage was obtained. The men of the
moving force were to see only about 100 inhabitants of the North at missions and trading posts during their 3,100-mile trek. The following day,
Werier of the *Winnipeg Tribune* flew over the force at Seal River, 42 miles
from Churchill, in an RCAF *Norseman*. He was also flown to Baker Lake to
witness the expedition's arrival.

It had not been possible, however, to assign journalists to the force for
the duration of the 81-day journey. In order to provide coverage throughout the expedition, army public relations in Ottawa assigned Lieutenant
R.W. (Bob) Morton, a still photographer from Port Arthur, Ontario;
Sergeant Fred Way, a writer from Ottawa, and Sergeant C.R.J. Racine,
a cinematographer, also of Ottawa, to the moving force. They sent stories
by army wireless to either Churchill or Edmonton and, when possible,
shipped exposed film aboard RCAF aircraft flying supplies to the expedi-

tion. Canadian Press transmitted stories of reporters from membership newspapers to media throughout Canada.

Once the ground force left Churchill, I failed to arrange for a steady flow of information from the PR people with the ground force. I did manage to obtain some information through reports, but these were mostly of a technical nature. The root of the problem was that I had not requested the directorate of army public relations in Ottawa to provide me with details of their PR plan.

The start of the exercise did receive excellent coverage, but after that, newspaper and radio accounts were scarce. I saw little of the copy Fred Way wrote and a few of Bob Morton's photos.

I did, however, make an effort to inform a special public: the business community of Winnipeg. I was able to provide the *Activist* magazine of the Winnipeg Chamber of Commerce with a three-instalment account of the trek. Following are a few excerpts:

Camp at midday, 3 May 1946. Because of the milder temperature, the expedition travelled by night and slept by day. In sleeping bags: W. Rouse and Captain. W. Black; at back: Craftsman A. Disley (left) and Private Bill Wilson.
Courtesy National Archives of Canada, PA 167257.

Answers to Canada's biggest interrogation mark, the vast wastes of the Arctic northland, are being sought by members of the Canadian Army, the Royal Canadian Air Force and civilian scientists of Exercise Muskox. Upon the findings of this first expedition, which is now advancing over the first third of its 3,100-mile trek, may test the speed with which this territory is opened up to the economic field on a far greater scale than at present.

While both English and American observers are accompanying the moving force, it is entirely a Canadian venture ...

Constructed for the invasion of Norway, the army's snowmobiles may prove to be the answer to the north country's problem of surface travel. Armour has been removed from the original model and a cab substituted to protect the driver and three passengers ...

Arctic surface travel is complicated, not only by the frozen wastes of winter, but the spring break-up conditions. The snowmobile is of amphibious design and its possibilities during the spring break-up will be tested to the limit during the later portion of the trek ...

Specially designed Arctic clothing of several varieties is being tested and results will be passed on to appropriate authorities. It may be that as a result of Exercise Muskox, men who follow Canada's trap lines will in future be wearing more comfortable clothing and eating such delicacies as doughnuts.

The second article drew attention to serious problems met by the ground forces, including poor visibility, strain on mechanics "who cannot, like the Eskimo, throw their means of transportation a frozen fish and expect good results," overheated vehicles, excessive fuel consumption, and maps lacking detail.

The third article summarized the force's accomplishments.

Just what can be said of the force's accomplishments at this date? The most pointed answer is the men of

> Muskox have travelled by mechanical surface vehicle over approximately 3,000 miles of sub-Arctic and Arctic territory in 81 days. Allowing for weaknesses in the snowmobile, which were expected, the vehicle has proven its ability to travel over long distances in the frozen wastes ... some form of vehicle of this type, suitable for year-round travel in snow and mud, has a definite place in this country ...
>
> ... the exercise ... demonstrated that properly equipped men with little experience in the north but under proper guidance can live and travel in the north.

The article concluded with the force's struggle to advance in spring through snow, water, ice, and mud. Edmonton newspapers, radio stations, and Canadian Press gave extensive coverage on completion of the exercise when the soldiers, scientists, and Penguins of the moving force arrived 6 May in Edmonton by train.

The moving force paraded down Jasper Avenue to the Edmonton Armouries, where they were welcomed by Lieutenant-Governor J.R. Bowlen. Before leaving for Ottawa, the scientists and soldiers were also guests at a civic banquet.

In a final interview with journalists, Lieutenant-Colonel Baird said, "Muskox has successfully carried out its broad aims to prove men and machines against northern conditions and to gather scientific data." PR for the exercise's conclusion was planned and executed by Major A. Stirton, the army PRO in Edmonton.

However coverage didn't end until some five months after the exercise when cinecameraman Sergeant Racine's footage was released on the commercial theatre circuit after production of a film, *White Safari*, was completed by the National Film Board of Canada. The film's release allowed for a unique PR opportunity.

Early in March, when Reverend William James, a clergyman at Baker Lake, heard the Muskox force was expected, he sent word by dog-team for an Eskimo mother, Nannuk, and her eight-year-old son, Kooyak, to come to Baker Lake. The boy suffered from two club feet and without treatment his survival in the Arctic was questionable. Mother and son lived in a tiny settlement at Back River, west of Baker Lake.

The two were at Baker Lake when the Muskox force arrived. Permission was received from the RCMP to fly them via RCAF aircraft to Churchill and on to Winnipeg. It was their first visit to the south.

When *White Safari* was released, the manager of the Metropolitan Theatre in Winnipeg asked the army if an exhibition of Arctic equipment could be displayed in the lobby. A Penguin and some Arctic clothing were provided.

My cameraman, Sergeant Pete Gordon, and I discussed the possibility of private screening for Nannuk, who had been away from the Arctic for almost five months. Pete suggested using infra-red film and flashbulbs to photograph Nannuk as she watched the film. In the darkness of the theatre, the action of the infrared flashbulbs would not be visible, so the camera's operation would not interfere with her viewing experience. To solve the language problem – Nannuk spoke no English – I obtained the agreement of the Hudson's Bay Company to supply two employees who spoke her language.

Nannuk agreed to attend the private screening and the theatre manager arranged for invitations, which included Winnipeg journalists.

Accompanied by a nurse from the Children's Hospital, Nannuk saw her first movie. The event was a success – not only from a PR viewpoint, but also for Nannuk. Asked by one interpreter what she thought of the film, the reported reply was: "Cocking her head to the side, she replied shyly, 'Yes, I liked it very much.' Then she added that she would be glad to return to her homeland, a comment which hinted that the film had stirred thoughts of her family."

Pete Gordon's photos of Nannuk couldn't have been better. The documentary began with a scene of a parka-clad figure walking across the white desert over which snow was rapidly blowing; they were signs of a blizzard beginning. Nannuk frowned. When she saw her own people, she broke into a smile. For Nannuk, however, the highlight was a scene which captured some Eskimo children cavorting with dogs near the entrance to an igloo. It was the only time she laughed.

The effectiveness of Gordon's still photos was apparent by the treatment given to them by Winnipeg's two daily newspapers, the *Free Press* and the *Tribune*. Both positioned the pictures and story on their front pages, the *Free Press* using six, two-column pictures down the front page and, above this, a three-column picture of Nannuk as she prepared to leave the hospital for the theatre. Soon after the screening, Nannuk and Kooyak returned home to the Arctic. The child's club feet had been corrected.

Winnipeg's Metropolitan Theatre received the top Hollywood award for promotion of a short film in 1946.

Weeks after the exercise, I was still thinking about the PR results and what they had taught me. Most of what I learned arose from mistakes that I had made. The biggest shortcoming was my failure to make full use of communications on three counts.

First, I had incorrectly assumed that heavy static made for inferior Arctic radio communications. As a result, I did not attempt to arrange with individual radio stations or networks periodic interviews as the moving force progressed across the Arctic. The interviews could have brought the reality of the exercise, its soldiers, airmen, and scientists into the living rooms of Canadian homes.

Secondly, the three articles I wrote for the *Activist* could have received much broader distribution. Chamber of Commerce magazines do not compete with one another. Therefore I could have submitted the article to each Canadian Chamber of Commerce publication, which would have resulted in a large segment of Canada's business community learning about the exercise.

Perhaps the best of the few good things I did was to release problems, slight and serious, that surfaced in the exercise. They included accounts of poor visibility, the snowmobiles' excessive fuel consumption, unsatisfactory snow goggles, and the inefficiencies of the Arctic clothing. In all subsequent exercises in which I participated for over 23 years, reporters were told at the outset that the purpose of an exercise was to find weaknesses. If none were found, the exercise was probably a failure.

Part of the problem may have been that the principle of integrating the PR planning with the operational plan had not been given enough emphasis.

Finally, I failed to follow up with the results of the exercise's scientific findings, which I attribute to distraction from the aftermath of the Pacific War. I had begun to work on this problem, just before planning for Muskox began.

CHAPTER 3

THE HONG KONG COURTS MARTIAL

I had no sooner begun preparatory PR work on Muskox when Brigadier Morton introduced me to a new problem about mid-October 1945. It was my first unpleasant story.

Morton called me to his office, where he asked me if the assistant judge advocate general (AJAG) of our headquarters (the army's lawyer in Prairie Command) had told me about the three non-commissioned officers – two Britons and a Canadian – who were on their way to Winnipeg, where they would be detained pending an investigation. I replied that I had not been informed. The brigadier was not pleased, but he gave me a short briefing. He then called the AJAG to say I was en route to his office and that he was to provide me with all the details.

Two British servicemen, one a sergeant-major, the other a sergeant, and a Canadian company sergeant-major of the Winnipeg Grenadiers, had been ordered detained because of accusations that included manslaughter, assaulting subordinates, stealing and misusing Red Cross parcels, and collaborating with the Japanese. An investigation was underway which would determine whether there was both substance to the accusations and sufficient evidence to warrant courts martial.

The major problem was that the witnesses were widely scattered, some abroad. It was anticipated the decision concerning the possible courts martial would not be forthcoming for several months. (In the end, it took about five-and-a-half months to determine that charges would be laid.)

The battle for Hong Kong and the subsequent conditions under which Canadian soldiers were held prisoner must be appreciated in order to understand the courts martial and my solution to the PR problem.

In September, Britain received a positive response to a request that Canada provide two infantry battalions to reinforce Hong Kong. The Japanese had not declared war and British authorities, military and civilian, believed reinforcement action would have a deterrent effect on Japan. The Royal Victoria Rifles of Montreal and the Winnipeg Grenadiers were chosen for the assignment. Both had just returned to Canada after serving as garrison troops in Newfoundland and Jamaica, respectively. It was expected they would continue the garrison role in Hong Kong.

The units, 1,975 strong, arrived in Hong Kong on 16 November 1941. In the three weeks before the Japanese attacked, the Canadians familiarized themselves with a static role, defending Hong Kong beaches and coordinating with British and Indian troops.

Hong Kong was devoid of air support. Total aircraft numbered only six. What was perhaps even worse was the sorry state of artillery weapons, which were few and, in some cases, obsolete. The fixed guns faced seaward and could not be traversed because the British authorities anticipated that any Japanese attack would come across the strait separating the mainland from the island.

Compounding the lack of air support and weak artillery was the failure to recognize the quality and determination of the Japanese units. They stormed down the mainland on 7 December and their air force attacked Hong Kong shortly after blasting Pearl Harbor. There would be no U.S. assistance for Hong Kong.

Only those who have been under prolonged shellfire and aerial bombardment can appreciate the impact. For those in Hong Kong, it was even worse knowing their capacity to fight back was seriously restricted by lack of air power and adequate fire support. However, fight back they did.

The Royal Rifles were cut off and three attempts to break out of the encirclement resulted in more casualties. For a period of eight days, what little sleep and cold food they obtained was snatched in weapons slits, a narrow trench for two soldiers.

The Grenadiers launched a drive on December 18 for Jardine's Lookout and Mount Butler. One company was virtually wiped out trying to seize both objectives. Another company delayed the Japanese for three days, but were eventually forced to surrender on 22 December.

During this battle, Company Sergeant-Major J.R. Osborne of A-Company, and a veteran of the Great War of 1914–18, earned Canada's first Victoria Cross of the Second World War. After holding Mount Butler for three hours with a detachment of Winnipeg Grenadiers, they were forced to withdraw and establish a new position. The Japanese pressure continued. Osborne caught and threw enemy grenades back at the

Japanese. When one fell beyond his reach, he threw himself on top of it, thereby shielding his men. He died instantly.

After 17 1/2 days of fighting, the two Canadian units had 23 officer and 267 other rank casualties. The Japanese ended the battle Christmas Day with a series of ghastly atrocities, including murder and rape, primarily against the patients and staff at the Hong Kong hospital.

The enemy then slammed the door of the tomb shut. It wasn't a merry Christmas. The Canadians had been captured by an enemy whose culture bore no relation whatsoever to that of Europe or Canada. Until the Japanese surrender in 1945, only dribbles of information leaked from the tomb.

Shortly before the Japanese surrender, my former commanding officer in northwest Europe, Brigadier R.S. (Dick) Malone, was assigned to take a small Canadian Armed Forces mission to visit the Pacific theatre of operations in advance of the arrival of a Canadian force. The mission was to carry out general liaison work and plan Canadian press coverage. Malone was accompanied to the Philippines by Major Colin McDougall and Lieutenant-Commander Peter MacRitchie. McDougall, a combat cameraman, was wounded during the assault landing at Anzio, Italy, and went through the northwest Europe campaign. His film made a significant contribution to Canada's photographic record of the Second World War.

Before leaving Canada, Malone had indications that the Americans wished to finish off the Japanese by themselves without help from Britain or Canada. Now that the war had ended in Europe, more U.S. men, weapons, and supplies could be poured into the Pacific theatre. While en route to the Phillipines, Malone and his two companions experienced, first-hand, the bitterness and resentment felt by many soldiers in the Pacific over the European theatre having priority. During an island stopover, the three Canadians visited an officers' mess. Their uniforms were mistaken for British uniforms by a small group of American war correspondents and the U.S. Army officers sitting within earshot. This group began referring to the "Brits" in a series of foul names, much to Malone's embarrassment. Suddenly Colin McDougall was on his feet and growled, "If we were that kind of people, we'd be into you so fast it would make your head swim!"

A brief silence ensued, and then the response: "Migawd! Canadians!"

On arrival in the Philippines, Malone reported to MacArthur's chief public relations officer. This officer doubted MacArthur would have the time to see Malone, so Malone gave him the letters he carried from each of the heads of Canada's Armed Forces and the prime minister and requested that they be passed on to the general.

Meanwhile, he spent time getting to know American, Australian, and British war correspondents, from whom he learned that wireless transmission and censorship for the press were concentrated at MacArthur's headquarters. Getting stories out quickly meant staying close by the headquarters, far back of the fighting troops. Malone was also able to obtain the views of Bill Stewart of Canadian Press, who had covered operations in Italy and northwest Europe – where I had conducted him – before he was dispatched to the Pacific.

Australian copy had to be transmitted from MacArthur's headquarters to San Francisco, then back again across the Pacific to Australia. This more than doubled the cost of transmission and created long delays in publication. The result was that the Australian Army never received the credit it was due for the long and intensive fighting it waged to a victorious conclusion in the Pacific.

Subsequently, Malone and McDougall were involved in the Japanese surrender ceremony aboard the USS *Missouri* in Tokyo Bay on 2 September 1945.

Malone had received direction from Ottawa to locate as quickly as possible the Canadian POWs and provide relief and speedy evacuation, all the while keeping Ottawa informed. He learned the Canadian prisoners were spread from Hong Kong to Tokyo. He obtained an accurate account of the prisoners from Prince Tokugawa, who worked in the Japanese Embassy in Ottawa when Malone was a journalist in the Parliamentary Press Gallery before the war. He then cabled the list to Ottawa.

Ottawa dispatched a rehabilitation team to Manila. Doctors in the Pacific urged Malone to delay the return of the freed troops to Canada so they could undergo rehabilitation before meeting their families. Many weighed less than 100 pounds. They needed food, medical care, psychiatric counselling, and briefings about the changed world which they were about to re-enter. After setting up the rehabilitation transit camp in Manila, Malone returned to civilian life.

As a result of the liberation of the Canadian troops, the dribble of information since 1941 quickly became a flood. The information was shocking.

The clash of cultures had an overwhelming impact on the imprisoned Canadians. The Japanese did not believe soldiers should surrender; rather, they should prefer death. The small number of Japanese taken prisoner in the Pacific indicates the vast majority of them practised what they believed. This undoubtedly influenced, but did not excuse, their attitude and treatment of Allied prisoners.

Malone reported at the first prison camp he reached that "the men were in rags, their bodies emaciated and discoloured with sores." Some were too weak to stand and many were suffering mentally.

At Oeyama Camp, the worst of the prisons, the Japanese commandant had warned the Canadians they were subject to Japanese military law, which included "Binta" – slapping and punching subordinates. There was plenty of that, including slapping and punching by British and Canadian non-commissioned officers (NCOs) of other rank Canadians. It was this accusation, among others, which ultimately led to the Hong Kong courts martial.

The camp hospital was a filthy hut with vermin-infested blankets and, in Japanese style, a mat on the floor for a bed. There were no sheets. The prisoners talked about food "all the time," and it was a common occurrence for men to keel over due to vitamin deficiencies. Medical supplies were scarce and sedatives almost non-existent.

Canadian prisoners of war aboard HMCS *Prince Robert*, near a suburb of Hong Kong, August 1945, following their release from a Japanese POW camp.
Courtesy National Archives of Canada, PA 145521.

Men were forced to work in ill-fitting boots; as a result, many lost toes. One soldier was forced to work in boots with a quarter-inch of bone of one toe sticking out of the flesh. When it was discovered that the men resorted to cutting blankets to wrap the strips around their feet, they were forced to run a gauntlet of Japanese soldiers, where they were kicked and beaten. Following this, they were denied their evening meal and forced to stand at attention on the parade ground virtually all night. All of the prisoners were paraded and forced to watch the gauntlet of punishment.

The food became progressively worse. Men were afraid to go into the hospital where patients were dying of dysentery, pellagra, and beriberi. Men were also dying of starvation.

There were accusations of theft and misuse of Red Cross food parcels. Mainly because of poor conditions, four officers and 125 other ranks died in the Hong Kong camps. Four of these soldiers were shot without trial by the Japanese when they were recaptured after escaping. At Oeyama, one doctor had treated 500 cases of diphtheria, 3,000–4,000 cases of dysentery, and more than 300 cases of malaria.

From January 1943 onwards, one officer and 1,183 other ranks were taken to Japan to work in the mines. One hundred and thirty-five of them died. Of the 1,975 Canadian soldiers who sailed from Vancouver, 555 never returned home.

Despite the horrors of the situation, many prisoners continued their resistance to the enemy. An underground information system was operated and there were many incidents where Canadians instigated sabotage, especially in the Japanese shipbuilding industry. One method was to set a fire by means of a candle surrounded by flammable material, which would catch fire when it burned down after the prisoners had left the construction site.

At home, Brigadier Morton was concerned how the story should be handled and passed to journalists. He was worried about the impact coverage would have on the non-commissioned officers under investigation. It seemed unfair for them to be submitted to charges that had not been substantiated. As well, the arguments and rumours would continue throughout the extended time it would take for the court to give its verdict. It would be even more devastating if the court decided the evidence gathered did not merit courts martial.

I had followed the newspaper reports about the liberated prisoners and had also played a small part in their repatriation. In addition to the rehabilitation transit camp in Manila, the army established a second camp on the west coast of British Columbia. Through Dick Malone, now back at the *Winnipeg Free Press*, and Carlyle Allison, editor of the *Winnipeg Tribune*, I arranged to have the west coast transit camp supplied with copies of the two Winnipeg daily newspapers. Army headquarters in Ottawa arranged for the Montreal dailies for the Royal Victoria Rifles. As such, I did have some details of hardships suffered by the Canadian troops and I had anticipated the brigadier's concern towards presentation of the story to journalists. The environment when the war with Japan ended, the suffering borne by the troops, the extended time it would take the Court of Inquiry to act – all influenced my advice.

My response was to ask his permission to visit the two newspapers, as well as radio stations, and present them with the known facts. I would ask that they not use the story until, and if, charges were laid. The three NCOs being detained undoubtedly had been through almost four years of living hell; it would have been unfair to try and handle the story when it comprised accusations and rumours. I proposed that the Winnipeg media be given the guarantee that they would be the first to be told when and if the courts martial would be held and, if they were, our headquarters would provide every possible facility and assistance to cover the trials. Therefore, they would be the first to publish the story.

I started my media tour with Carlyle Allison. I explained the brigadier's concerns. Allison's first question concerned the *Free Press*: what were they doing? I told him I was visiting the *Free Press* next and would telephone their reply to him. Dick Malone agreed to hold the story. I then told Allison and Malone that I'd approach the radio stations and relay the results. All were promised that if the courts martial were to be held, they would be the first to be told.

The result of my visits was unanimous agreement by the Winnipeg media to withhold the story until formal charges were laid. I then informed Major Hector Stewart, assistant director of public relations (army) in Ottawa, of the Winnipeg media's reaction and the promise made.

I then turned back to work on Exercise Muskox.

About 2 or 3 March 1945, Stewart telephoned me to say that the Court of Inquiry had recommended the courts martial be held. The trials were essential. Military law prohibits the striking of another rank. Had the British and Canadian NCOs not struck their own men, the Japanese officers and soldiers would have been more severe. What took so much time was determining if the evidence concerning the accusations of manslaughter, stealing, abuse of Red Cross parcels, and collaborating with the Japanese merited holding the courts. He added that the War Office in

London was planning to release the story the next day. Since the major British dailies were morning newspapers, the story would break in London several hours before it would in Winnipeg. I was furious.

"Hec," I said, "if that happens, you'll have my resignation on your desk first thing in the morning. I'll be of no further use to army public relations." Stewart requested that I just sit tight until he looked into what he could do.

The next day, he called to say London had agreed the story should be released first in Winnipeg and was sending me a news release. My promise was upheld.

When delivering the release to the media the next day, I informed them a special briefing on the courts martial would be provided and the differences between the military and civilian courts explained. The briefing was held prior to 11 March when the first trial began.

The courts martial were held in a wartime army hut. A special table was made available for journalists and there was space for about 100 spectators. Nearby, a workroom, typewriters, and telephones were provided for the reporters. The two British NCOs were tried by a court composed of British officers, while the Canadian appeared before Canadian officers.

The British regimental sergeant-major was eventually acquitted of all five charges of assaulting subordinates. The British sergeant was acquitted on all 11 charges. The eight charges of assaulting fellow prisoners that were subject to confirmation by the war office were subsequently quashed. The Canadian Company sergeant-major faced 19 charges. He was acquitted on 11 of them. Eight charges alleging he struck or assaulted other POWs were subject to confirmation by National Defence Headquarters, Ottawa. He received a reprimand.

At the outset of the courts martial, the British Military Mission based in Washington requested they be provided with all print stories published in Winnipeg. At the conclusion of the trials, our headquarters received a letter of thanks from the mission, stating that it was the best balanced reporting of courts martial they had seen. The Winnipeg media deserved the compliment.

The courts martial reinforced a PR principle I had learned in wartime: Be the first, if possible, to inform the media completely and accurately about an unpleasant incident, no matter how embarrassing. Reporters prefer to get information from official sources if they know from experience it will be accurate and complete. If the official source refuses to cooperate, they'll dig out the information from other sources, which may lead to inaccuracies.

A public relations practitioner's integrity – even if earned over a period of time – is fragile. If a promise is made, it must be kept. Reporters must learn from the beginning that you'll provide the facts and the details they need, when needed. By providing the reporters the facilities they need, you contribute to the quality of the reportage.

The courts martial also taught me that one well-handled, unpleasant story will do more to establish good media relations than a hundred promotional stories. Whenever I was assigned a new posting, I almost prayed for an unpleasant story that would give me an opportunity to quickly establish sound media relations. To do this, you must have the willing support of your masters. My superior officers, without exception, provided that support. The other key officers had a responsibility to keep me informed. The judge advocate general never failed to keep me in the picture after the courts martial incident.

This requirement to keep the public relations executive informed applies also to the private and public sectors.

From Malone's experience in the Pacific, I concluded that a national force operating in an alliance must be able to provide communications and security reviews for the correspondents it serves. However, I believe it would take almost another war for me to again recommend that a story be held back. Certainly, in peacetime it leads to disaster.

As the trial came to an end, I received direction from Ottawa to coordinate the news release announcing the award of a posthumous Victoria Cross to Company Sergeant-Major John Robert Osborne. I only wish I had known him.

CHAPTER 4

REDRAMP

The year 1950 was a vintage one for learning and experience. It began late in the winter with attendance at a three-and-a-half-month course at the United States Armed Forces Information School in Carlisle, Pennsylvania, not far from the capital of Harrisburg.

Carlisle Barracks is one of the oldest barracks in the United States. It is still equipped with the early cells and ankle-and-neck stockades in which British prisoners of war were clamped during the War of Independence.

The information officers course was attended by soldiers, sailors, marines, airmen, civil servants, RCAF Flight Lieutenant Al Marshall and me – the only two Canadians.

The information school was well equipped for its functions: teaching Armed Forces officers and selected civil servants how the media works, the problems journalists face, and how information officers could assist the media. The school had a newspaper plant, a radio station, and a television station, none of which broadcast a signal to the outside world. Every tutorial period, the students were divided into syndicates, each of which produced a newspaper, radio programs, and telecasts primarily with a news format.

Our first newswriting exercises revealed that we were not all amateurs. We were given a fact sheet containing detailed background. Our assignment was to shape a formal news story. In one exercise, the incident we were given took place on a major army base. A staff sergeant walking inside the base spotted an electric wire that had broken and fallen to the ground. Just then, a dog snapped at it and was knocked unconscious. The staff sergeant obtained a large stick, rolled the dog away from the wire, and carried the unconscious animal to the army medical centre where it was treated and later recovered.

One student's lead to the story, by far the best of the class, read: "A telephone pole today gained revenge on dogdom!" I was in fast company.

Each week, the school flew in prominent journalists, broadcasters, opinion analysts, cinematographers, and writers. Each speaker was tape-recorded and the resulting tape placed in an extensive library which also contained books, papers, and articles on public relations, public opinion, sociology, and psychology, as well as photographs and pertinent graphic art.

My only disappointment at Carlisle came just as I was leaving to return to Winnipeg. The school's commandant, Brigadier E.J. McGaw, who commanded U.S. airborne troops during the Arnheim Operation in the Second World War, asked me to come to his office. He told me Washington had asked Ottawa to loan me to the school for a two-year tour of duty to give the Commonwealth lectures and contribute to the journalism lectures. They had earmarked a two-storey, red brick, colonial-style married quarters for our family. Ottawa, however, declined the invitation. I never learned why.

As a result of the course, I discovered that I had American friends at U.S. Army (Europe) Headquarters in Frankfurt when I was posted to Germany in 1954. They provided repair services for our army cameras. Through them, I met the head of U.S. army public relations in Europe, Colonel Robert Shinn, who later became the deputy head of army public relations at the Pentagon when I was director of army PR in Ottawa. I have often speculated about what advantages might have arisen for our countries and services had Ottawa accepted General McGaw's invitation.

I picked up Colleen and the children in Toronto and we drove back to Winnipeg. We saw some early evidence of impending flood danger, swollen rivers and creeks, but we didn't recognize what it was forecasting.

The army gives each exercise a code name. The choice of Redramp for the Red River flooding was one of the few that failed to accurately describe the event at hand. While the flood would eventually do millions of dollars damage, it didn't have the characteristics of a rampage, such as the wild, thrashing, broiling destruction of the Mississippi in flood.

The flood was like the slow, relentless, threatening movement of a boa constrictor that had taken on the colouring of the environment and was winding itself around its victim as it tried to choke out Prairie life.

Shortly after I returned to Winnipeg Prairie Command Headquarters (the Military District No. 10 designation had been changed), I was called upon to provide assistance in fighting the advancing waters and in helping citizens and their threatened homes and livestock. Initially, the troops helped with dikes, evacuated patients from hospitals, and moved cattle to higher ground. The public relations task was to keep journalists informed of the army's activities and arrange assistance if they wanted to see those activities. It was not a difficult task.

About 7:30 a.m. on 6 May, a telephone call to my office changed the pace of activities. I answered, and a clipped voice said only, "Sunray, come."

"Yes, sir," I replied to my commander, Brigadier R.E.A. Morton. ("Sunray" was the wireless code for commander.)

On arriving from overseas after the war, I had served under his brother, Brigadier R.O.G. Morton. Both men were graduates of the Royal Military College at Kingston, Ontario. He was filled with nervous energy which snapped, crackled, and popped when things were quiet. He always seemed to stir up the pot for us if nothing was happening. His use of wireless procedure for telephone conversations, which kept us on our toes, was just one example. However, when excitement reigned, he became quiet, calm, and pensive.

After replying to "Sunray," I hurried to the floor above in the headquarters. Morton's office was directly above mine. On arrival, I was invited to sit down. The brigadier gave me a quick, precise briefing. Manitoba Premier D.L. Campbell had requested that the army take over command of flood control immediately. The brigadier was to set up Flood Control Headquarters in the Manitoba Legislative Buildings no later than noon that day. He had a meeting scheduled for 9:30 a.m. with the premier. He asked what I would need to carry out the overall responsibility for the public relations function. I requested 30 minutes to sort out my thoughts and then I would phone him.

I returned to my office and put my head in my hands. I had one secretary and a sergeant photographer, certainly not adequate staffing for the task ahead. Then I remembered that during the war we had recruited Tom Johnson of Manitoba's Travel and Publicity Bureau (MTPB) as a member of the Fort Osborne PR office. After the war, Tom moved east. The memory of him and the bureau saved the day. I phoned the brigadier, recommending he request the staff and facilities of the MTPB be placed at our disposal. It would be a 24-hour daily, seven-day-a-week job before the flood was brought under control and the threat of severe flooding ended. We would need all the help we could get. Before noon, a message from the brigadier ordered me to move to the legislative buildings and take over the MTPB.

The public relations task was to keep the Manitoba public informed, as well as the general public across Canada. The news agency wire services and the radio broadcasting networks distributed the news nationally and internationally. Flood Control Headquarters public relations was set up in the MTPB's offices in the legislative building.

A statement by Premier Campbell announced the appointment of Morton as directing officer of all relief work. A statement from Morton was also delivered to the media. It read: "The Red Cross will continue to handle all requests for assistance with personal problems, such as housing, feeding, evacuation, and first aid. Requests for material aid, such as sandbags, pumps, boats, working parties, et cetera, should be made to the director of flood relief."

Telephone numbers for the Red Cross and Flood Control Headquarters were provided. The statement continued: "All will appreciate that both material and labour resources are limited. Every effort will be made to allot these where they will do the most good for the greatest number of people."

Soldiers of the Princess Patricia's Canadian Light Infantry taking part in sandbagging operations in the Manitoba flood of 1950.
Courtesy National Archives of Canada, PA 138948.

Additional sailors, soldiers, and airmen joined the task of assisting Winnipeg's citizens fight the advancing waters. The navy manned pumps and boats, provided temporary accommodation for refugees, and assisted in repair work, including underwater tasks carried out by navy divers. The RCAF provided Canada's greatest airlift to that date, transporting millions of sandbags, pumps, and shovels. The airmen also worked on the dikes and provided signals operators.

The main tasks of the RCMP were carried out in the municipalities. They assisted in evacuating people, prevented looting, and provided information to Flood Control Headquarters.

Soldiers formed the bulk of the servicemen, most being employed on dike work, in addition to the Flood Control Headquarters staff. Army field engineers worked closely with city and municipal engineers. Signallers, ambulance men, military police, and medical staff also were provided.

By noon Saturday, Flood Control Headquarters and the PR office were established in the legislative building. The first three days were difficult. The first task was to build up the PR staff and establish an effective means of communicating information to the media. MTPB staff was augmented by RCAF and navy staff. Help was also obtained from civilian public relations practitioners in Winnipeg. I requested to Brigadier Morton that he hold a news conference each weekday at 10:30 a.m. (10:00 a.m. on Saturdays) to brief reporters and answer questions. This would give them enough time to write their stories and have them published the same day. He agreed.

It was Monday evening before I left the headquarters and returned to our apartment in Fort Osborne Barracks. I had not spoken to or seen Colleen – or slept for that matter – since early Thursday morning. On leaving the legislative building, I rolled into the front seat of an army jeep and said, "Take me home."

"Where's home, sir?" the driver asked.

"Building 22," I replied and fell sound asleep.

The driver awakened me when we reached the barracks. Colleen undressed me and tucked me into bed. I was back at headquarters Tuesday morning.

But the problems faced by some of my civilian friends were more formidable than lack of rest. They were not only desperately short of sleep, but they were building dikes and attempting to control the rising water level in their homes by trying to keep the water level below the basement ceiling. Residents with flooded basements were being warned by army and

Brigadier R.E.A. Morton (at left of map) briefs the Joint Flood Control
Committee, comprised of military and government members. Daily briefings
were also provided for newspaper and radio reporters.
Courtesy National Archives of Canada, PA 128773.

civilian engineers not to try to keep the basements dry, but to allow the
water to rise while holding the water level below the ceiling. One civilian
ignored this advice and the basement wall on one side of his home col-
lapsed from the outside water pressure and the whole house canted.

At 4:30 p.m., I attended the daily meetings of the Flood Control
Committee chaired by Morton and held at Flood Control Headquarters.
This committee was made up of representatives from the province, the
police, the urban municipalities of Greater Winnipeg, including their
mayors, as well as city engineering departments, the railways, the Red
Cross, and the Women's Volunteer Bureau. Either Premier Campbell or
Deputy Premier Eric Willis attended each meeting.

The daily news conference opened with the intelligence officer delivering the current situation in Winnipeg and the urban areas. Brigadier Morton was the official spokesperson and he called on specialists of the headquarters for their reports. The provincial Department of Mines and Resources furnished flood forecasts. Morton was the ideal man to handle these morning conferences, as he was well-skilled at answering reporters' queries.

At the height of the flood, 40 to 60 Canadian, U.S., and European journalists attended the daily conferences. This dwindled down to four Winnipeg journalists when the waters began to recede. The public relations office acted as a message centre for the journalists and provided copies of news releases. They were usually kept to a minimum, as the bulk of the information was provided at the morning news conference. Questions from individual journalists were fielded by myself or those on duty on a 24-hour, seven-day-a-week basis. If we didn't have an answer, it could quickly be obtained by walking down the hall to the operations room.

On 7 or 8 May, the first serious public relations problem arose. In emergencies involving the public at large, a small lunatic fringe is all too often stimulated to create unnecessary panic. During Redramp, false information about supposed breaks in dikes and the need for additional workers was telephoned to Winnipeg radio stations, who were invaluable in quickly transmitting information to the public. These false reports were creating frustration and confusion. The requests were being prefaced by the statement: "This is Flood Control Headquarters." This threat to effective operations was quickly ended by using code words, such as "green belt," between the media offices and Flood Control Headquarters public relations.

Soon after Morton's appointment, I recommended to him that he speak to the citizens of Manitoba, to describe for them the situations they were facing. I was convinced the population was becoming increasingly nervous about the flood. I had also learned that CBC Winnipeg had arranged a local network to link the CBC station, CKY, with the four private Winnipeg stations. Morton agreed to do the broadcast ... if I wrote it. Involved deeply in operational matters, he did not have time to write it himself. I was confident I could do it, having heard him speak enough times to pick up his style. I wrote a version for him, which he made his own. He was scheduled to be on the air for 10 minutes, from 9:30 to 9:40 p.m.

Delayed by operations at headquarters, Morton, accompanied by me and with little time to spare, sped in an army staff car to CKY where we were met at curbside by three of the station's anxious CKY executives. An elevator was being held in the lobby for us. We rushed into it and rode to the studio floor. Morton sat down in the studio with four minutes to air. I went to the control room and watched him through the window. He was calmly scanning his script when the announcer introduced him.

"Ladies and gentlemen," he began, "as you no doubt know by now, the Canadian Army has recently been asked by the Province of Manitoba to assume control of the flood situation in this province. At present, of course, this means the serious flooding of Red River Valley from the American border down to Lake Winnipeg. I have been designated as director of the control. I would like it to be understood by all that while the army has been appointed the predominate partner of the three fighting services on this occasion, we are cooperating together – RCN, RCAF and Canadian Army – as we customarily do in peace or war."

After listening for about two minutes, I said to myself, "My God, another Roosevelt."

Brigadier R.E.A. Morton tells the citizens of Winnipeg and Manitoba what they are facing in the flood of 1950. A network of all the radio stations in Winnipeg was organized by the CBC. Morton's periodic broadcasts were from CKY, the local station.
Courtesy Manitoba Archives.

Morton sounded as if he were talking to me alone. Members of the listening public reacted as I did.

His speech continued:

> The appointment of the Army as control in no way sub-stitutes martial law for civil law in this emergency, and you might like to know briefly how we are organized to work ... the basic principles are cooperation and coordi-nation ...
>
> I admit frankly that we may make mistakes, but we are really trying and, after all, have only been functioning since 10:15 a.m. yesterday ... I must say the real attitude of cooperation displayed is inspiring. The press and radio stations, such vital units in our lives today, are a great source of help to us all ...
>
> The situation is undoubtedly serious and do not let this pleasant weekend weather hide this fact from us. To save possible serious damage to our city, we must build and maintain essential dikes. You can all help if you follow these requests:
>
> a) Don't panic, but take a serious view of the situation.
>
> b) Obey all instructions that will be issued from time to time by this Committee.
>
> c) When citizens are asked to help, please do so.
>
> d) Listen to the radio for instructions and flood warnings.
>
> e) Be calm and patient in this serious emergency and help your less fortu-nate neighbour who may be tem-porarily in distress.

"The good Lord helps those who help themselves." May I conclude by suggesting that in this, our hour of trouble,

we all unite in asking Him to succour those in danger
and distress from the flood waters.

When the brigadier finished speaking, the switchboards of all five
radio stations lit up like Christmas trees. The general sense of what the
callers were saying was, "Thanks, now we have a better idea of what we're
facing."

In retrospect, I think the manner in which the brigadier spoke to the
public was as important as what he said. He told listeners the true situation. He displayed sincerity, confidence, and calmness. The clarity of his
address couldn't have been better. In addition, they were receiving the
information from the soldier who had overall responsibility for Redramp.
For me, it was like discovering a public relations diamond mine.

After the broadcast, CKY and other station managers asked that the
brigadier speak to the public on a regular basis. He agreed to do so, as
long as it did not interfere with flood operations.

The Flood Relief Committee's daily meetings were the major means
of civilian–military coordination of policy and operational information.
From the beginning, Morton realized the necessity of being able to move
heavy equipment to where it was needed, regardless of which level of civilian government owned it. In the initial stages, this created the only resistance to cooperation that developed during Redramp. The politicians
wanted to retain heavy equipment in their own jurisdictions in the event
it would be needed for sudden emergency.

To solve this and other problems, I recommended that a court
reporter be assigned to record all discussions and decisions of the Flood
Relief Committee. Morton could use this written record when formulating his operational orders. As well, copies could be made for civilian
authorities and organizations. With the aid of the provincial attorney general's department, I obtained a court reporter.

The existence of a verbatim record of the committee's discussions and
decisions would ensure that the elected representatives would carefully
weigh their responses and decisions on issues which affected more con-
stituencies than their own. If, as a result of their decisions, recriminations
arose, the record, if necessary, would provide the facts.

At the first meeting the reporter attended, I noticed that a stranger
had joined the civilian group of advisors. They sat in chairs positioned
along the walls of the room along with the military advisors. The elected
representatives – including the premier – and the brigadier were seated at
the boardroom table. The meeting was underway for about two or three

minutes when the stranger left his seat and walked up to the premier's side. He leaned over and whispered in Campbell's ear, then returned to his seat. When the brigadier paused in his opening remarks, Premier Campbell took the floor and said, "I see a record of our meeting is being kept, Mr. Brigadier." (The use of "Mister" amused us.) "I would hope that this record will be kept confidential."

Morton had anticipated the question and replied, "The record being kept will form the basis of my operations orders which must be based on the policies decided upon here and also the information we obtain from all the organizations represented on this committee. The record will be kept confidential. I am confident my public relations officer will release only that information vital for the public to receive." The brigadier then continued with the agenda while I silently glowed with delight. No further difficulties arose over the moving of heavy equipment.

As I was walking down the hallway to the MTPB offices after the meeting, a voice behind me said softly, "You SOB!"

I turned to face the voice. It was the stranger whom I noticed in the committee meeting, a slim, dark-haired young man with his hands thrust into the back pockets of his trousers and a broad smile on his lips. We were in front of my office. I invited him in and asked him what the problem was.

"You've got us on record and you know it," he said, adding, "I would have done the same thing in your place."

He then introduced himself as John de B. Payne, head of public relations for Hudson's Bay House, corporate headquarters of the Hudson's Bay Company. He had been assigned to help Premier Campbell with public relations for the duration of Redramp. It was the beginning of a pleasant and effective relationship that benefitted the military and the civilian governments.

It didn't take John long to swing into action. Premier Campbell broadcasted a report on the local CBC network 11 May and made a series of subsequent reports to the public. At the 12 May committee meeting, he said, "The press have not been in attendance at these meetings, and I think that is all to the good, and that it is the proper system. It is understood that the confidential nature of these discussions will be respected by all who are here. But we in government are getting some repercussions. I might say that we at least should be making some statements on some of these matters. We have been so anxious to maintain the confidential nature of these discussions and to leave them to the proper authorities that we have hesitated to do that.

Front page of the *Winnipeg Tribune*, 10 May 1950.
Courtesy Manitoba Archives.

"However," he continued, "I think there is a field in which we are very happy indeed to clear with both the brigadier's General Committee and Brigadier Malone's Planning Committee, so that something can be said to the public."

The Planning Committee had been created by Morton when he invited Brigadier Malone to form a committee of strong, capable civilians to plan for the worst possible situation – the entire evacuation of Winnipeg – while Morton continued the day-to-day battle with the flood. Malone was ideally qualified for the complex task. During the war, he had graduated from the army staff college, which sharpened his natural planning ability.

In a period of five days, Malone and his committee had completed a first draft of the detailed evacuation plan covering food, supplies, equipment, depots, provost tasks, engineers' tasks, evacuation methods to be followed, manpower resources, emergency shelters, medical services, communications, and transportation, including a trucking pool. Watching him work stirred memories; he had been my commanding officer during the northwest Europe campaign.

While many civilian members of the Planning Committee were aware of Malone's plan, its details were not publicized for fear of creating panic. However, every opportunity was seized to encourage Winnipeg residents to leave the city for non-threatened summer homes and the safe homes of relatives and friends inside and outside the province. The brigadier emphasized evacuation in the daily news conference. The encouragement was effective. Although it was impossible to record an absolutely accurate number of residents who left the city, an effort was made to achieve some count of passengers of vehicles, aircraft, and trains. In one period of four days, 48,900 people were counted. By 14 May, two-thirds of the hospital patients in Winnipeg had been evacuated. By 16 May, it was estimated that 90,000 had moved out; by 20 May, 106,000.

However, a change in the weather, from rain to sunshine, resulted in a disturbing reduction in the flow of evacuees out of Winnipeg. The policy was to continue to urge citizens to evacuate. Morton did so in each of his broadcasts until after 20 May. There was concern about the impact that would take place if a 600-square-mile flood-created lake in the Morris area and another lake 500 square miles south of the international border began to spill water throughout the city. Additionally, the experts were uncertain as to what would happen if the Assiniboine River flooded. The objective of pressuring residents to leave their homes was to reduce substantially the size of the population. In the event the city went under, the fewer the number of citizens in the city, the less risk to life and the less complex the task of final evacuation would be for those fighting the flood. This evacuation policy resulted in the sole friction between me and the media, in this case Canadian Press (CP).

John Dauphinee was manager of the Winnipeg Bureau (he would later become head of Canadian Press). A dedicated journalist, he moved a mattress and bed clothes into the bureau where he remained throughout the entire critical period of the flood. Under Dauphinee's direction, CP had consistently done a competent job of reporting the emergency. It was my habit to monitor the radio newscasts personally, as well as to have members of the staff do additional listening.

Late one morning, I heard a newscast that quoted Canadian Press as reporting that the Red River had crested and would now start to recede. This would certainly reduce the flow of evacuees, which was not desired. The deadlines of both Winnipeg daily newspapers, the *Free Press* and the *Tribune*, were only minutes away; if this information was incorrect, I would not want it reported. I checked with the operations room at headquarters and was told they *did not* believe the Red River had crested.

That left me with a dilemma. If I phoned Dauphinee, I could expect an argument. Being the first to announce that the river had crested would be a major news scoop. If I became embroiled in an argument, the daily newspaper would surely hit the streets with the story and the flow of evacuees could slow to a trickle. I phoned the newspapers immediately, using the code word of the day, and reported that the river had not crested and that it was anticipated that it would continue to rise. The newspapers killed the CP story. I then phoned Dauphinee.

He was furious and wanted to know why I hadn't phoned him first. I explained my reasoning to him. He told me that he had obtained his information directly from Flood Control Headquarters. I responded that only a few minutes before placing my call to him, the operations room denied the crest had been reached and their analysis was that the river was still on the rise. I did not ask him to name his source, but I suspected an officer in the operations rooms whom I considered somewhat thick-headed. (Asking a journalist to name his source under such circumstances is a no-no.) Dauphinee demanded to see the brigadier. I arranged a meeting immediately, after briefing Morton on the day's events.

The meeting was serious and businesslike in tone. After Dauphinee registered his complaint, Morton said whoever had provided the information was wrong. It was believed that the river would continue its rise and it was important to reduce the numbers living in Winnipeg by as many as possible. He expressed his regret that Dauphinee was misinformed. The meeting ended satisfactorily for Flood Control Headquarters, but Dauphinee must have felt a great deal of frustration at the turn of events. I was never able to confirm my suspicions as to his source. To my relief – credibility-wise – the water rose for two more days.

The importance of the public relations function in an emergency cannot be overlooked, especially in this case. The Central Mortgage and Housing Corporation reported 8,581 houses completely flooded; 2,358 of these were flooded over the first floor. The 106,000 evacuees points to the effectiveness of the media and public relations functions.

Thousands of civilians, as well as those in uniform, worked on the dikes in foul and fair weather. At the height of the crisis, there were more than 5,000 members of the armed forces working at all levels with the civilian authorities. The navy had 650 officers and men operating 150 amphibious craft, evacuating the homeless, feeding livestock, rescuing the marooned, and operating 200 pumps. More than 3,600 soldiers worked on the dikes, patrolled roads and bridges, manned wireless sets, and managed thousands of tons of supplies and equipment. The RCAF airlifted in excess of one million pounds of equipment, including 1,200,000 sandbags, pumps, rubber boots, wireless sets, hospital cots, and blankets from across Canada and the United States. Additionally, they flew out 276 stretcher patients.

As the flood crest approached, John Payne stopped by my office to coordinate the announcement to the public that the danger had now passed. A few broadcasters had raised the subject, many expressing hope that the announcement would be made by Brigadier Morton. I explained that it was still too early to raise the subject, given that the brigadier was immersed in the day-to-day operations of the flood control.

Payne explained that the provincial government wanted to ensure the initial announcement would be made by civil authority – Premier Campbell. Throughout Redramp, Morton had meticulously been aware and respectful of the civil authority and the place of the military within the community. Knowing this, I told Payne that there was no doubt in my mind that the brigadier would prefer that the premier make the announcement. I told him I would speak to Morton. I then went on to observe that in the past week, some of the mayors and provincial authorities had been asking that the troops be retained well after the danger had passed and until all the evacuees had returned.

I knew the brigadier was prepared to hold some of the troops in Winnipeg once the crest had passed, but I was also aware that he and his unit commanders wanted to get the soldiers to their home bases where they could enjoy a brief respite before beginning summer training.

The decision was made quickly. Premier Campbell would make the initial announcement. Brigadier Morton would then broadcast his farewell along with his gratitude to all concerned, after which he would begin thinning out the troops.

Redramp was one of, if not the most, successful peacetime operation to that date involving civilians and the military at all three levels of government. In his farewell broadcast, Morton stressed the importance of the roles played by the Provincial Department of Public Works under George Collins, who acquired resources, and W.D. Hurst, Winnipeg's city engineer, who worked on dike construction, protection of utilities, and the railroads, which transported evacuees and patients.

The gradual withdrawal of the troops ended, for the armed forces, Operation Redramp. However, the army traditionally studies each of its operations and exercises to identify the lessons learned. No sooner had Redramp ended than Brigadier Morton recorded these lessons in an official report. Some are as follows:

> Redramp provided a useful insight into the reaction of the public of a large Canadian city threatened by (natural) disaster. The psychological effect of the steady and unpreventable rise of water over a considerable period of time was interesting.

> Each day ... I held a press conference for the 40 to 60 representatives from newspapers, broadcasting stations and syndicates. Our policy throughout was to give them the situation and all information possible at this conference or by special release at other times. We answered questions and held nothing back from them.

> A very important aspect of our work was our relations with the public. It was obviously necessary to have their confidence and support under existing circumstances and even more so if the situation had deteriorated and a large evacuation had become necessary.

> We were as frank and friendly as we could be and I think the "press" they gave us was very good.

Public relations proved very important during the flood. We gave it every consideration and it paid off. It is necessary to inform and quietly influence the public if you are to control them in the difficult and dangerous circumstances surrounding an emergency. The newspaper and radio were most helpful to us, but this pleasant situation might not always have been arrived at. Care should always be taken that at least one news sheet is published in a disaster. And that one radio station can keep to the air and also that the public can hear it.

The direct access to Brigadier Morton was essential to the success of the public relations function. Additionally, he readily agreed to meet the reporters daily, despite the obvious operational pressures. And he was an excellent spokesman.

The ideal situation is when the head of an organization has effective communications skills and the ability to think and act coolly under pressure. Morton also handled questions well and that Roosevelt-like voice held the attention of listeners and won their confidence.

This and the application of foresight is now more broadly accepted and implemented. Hospitals, oil and gas companies, railways, and chemicals companies now have emergency plans. Such organizations will deal with a crisis more effectively for applying such foresight. They will also experience more accurate and understanding reportage.

Subjectively, Redramp brought the realization and confidence I could operate under pressure. Morton taught me the importance of remaining calm. I considered the PR objective of effectively informing the populace a success. I attended all the meetings of the operations' groups and the PR office was located within a few yards of the operations room. I had learned a great deal and was identifying more clearly with PR principles I had learned during the war.

CHAPTER 5

MANITOBA'S 1953 POLIO EPIDEMIC

Seldom, if ever, will a PR practitioner be involved in a project that becomes highly personal. When it happens, you work with an intensity you never believed you could achieve. It happened to me during Manitoba's 1953 polio epidemic.

In the summer of 1953, Canada suffered its last polio epidemic, Manitoba being one of the hardest-hit provinces. The previous year, it had suffered a serious polio outbreak. The medical community and the province's citizens were hoping the scale of the new attack would be smaller. In mid-July, Dr. M.R. Elliott, deputy minister of health and welfare, in response to citizens' concerns, said there were no epidemic areas and hoped the incidence of cases would diminish before the usual peak period following the mid-summer hot weather. However, the desired conditions did not develop and the province and its citizens experienced a major disaster. By the end of August, there were 22 deaths. This was a far deadlier disaster than the 1950 flooding which had resulted in only one fatality.

For the armed forces, the army in particular, the fundamental difference between the two disasters was that the civilian medical community and the municipal and provincial governments were in command during the epidemic, whereas the army, air force, and navy provided assistance only when needed. Thus, my task as public relations officer of Prairie Command – which included Manitoba, Saskatchewan, and northwestern Ontario – was to keep newspapers, radio stations, and wire services informed about army activities. The task was not complex, but before the epidemic ended, PR principles had surfaced and a highly personal crisis developed. The flood, from a PR standpoint, had been much more difficult, but far less personal.

Medical authorities of the two governments provided the media with most of the information, including statistics. The command medical officer was Colonel C.G. Wood. He was in charge of medical assistance provided by the armed forces and, therefore, he was my main source of information. If the support the army provided was likely to raise media questions concerning medical aspects, an interview with Colonel Wood was arranged.

I provided less important information via telephone or fact sheet to the media. Other than the much-needed provision of nurses and orderlies, the only information about army support that I provided concerned the generators that were positioned beside the isolation hospital that would provide electricity for the iron lungs in the event the hospital's electrical system failed. Fortunately, it never did.

The air force provided information concerning the flights made to various points on the continent to pick up iron lungs.

As early as 16 July Dr. Elliott had noticed a serious problem developing: a shortage of nurses. Throughout the duration of the epidemic, the deputy minister and the medical community did a sound job of taking action to try and solve the problem and inform the media.

The Committee on Polio, created for the epidemic, made an urgent appeal for 16 registered and practical nurses for duty at Winnipeg's King George Hospital's polio wards. Winnipeg's medical health officer closed down the city's 12 child health centres to make more nurses available and the provincial health services released four public health nurses to do polio work. By 16 July Prairie Command had volunteered the services of three army nurses and two medical assistants for as long as they were needed.

The combined actions by the civilian medical community, the provincial government, and the army eased, but did not solve, the problem. However, the province had a reserve of equipment, including iron lungs, as a result of the polio attacks which took place in 1941.

I had an excellent source of assistance. The Prairie Command PR staff consisted of a secretary, Julie Le Doux, Sergeant Photographer Paul Tomlin, and me. It didn't take long to realize two things: 1) I would need knowledgeable PR help, because with more than two provinces to cover, I couldn't always be in the office; and 2) my secretary was not only capable of efficiently carrying out secretarial responsibilities, she also displayed a keen interest in the practice of PR. Her training in the function began shortly after she was assigned to the PR office.

Near the end of July, Colleen, the four children, and I left for a holiday at Star Lake, Manitoba, near the Ontario border. We were pleased to be able to take the children out of Winnipeg where, because of the population concentration, the number of polio cases was the largest in the province. By the end of July, Manitoba had more than 300 cases, the most severe ratio for a province in Canada. For about the same period the previous year, there had been 58 cases.

Three days before we were to return to Winnipeg, our seven-year-old daughter, Eileen, became ill. She was running a fever and suffering from headaches. There were no doctors nearby, so we decided to cut our holiday short and return to the city to our family doctor. On arriving in Winnipeg, we paused at my parents' home to inform them of our return. My mother saw us and came out to the curb as Colleen and I were getting out of the car.

"Colleen," she said, "I'm afraid I have terrible news. We have just learned that your mother has died." Elizabeth Clancy had lived in Montreal.

The news hit Colleen hard, but her concern for Eileen helped to divert some of the shock. I had always loved and respected Colleen's mother. She raised a family of five – four girls and a boy – almost single-handedly after her husband died at the early age of 44.

We told my parents about Eileen's illness and remained with them only long enough to telephone our family physician. We told the doctor we were leaving for our married quarters at Fort Osborne Barracks immediately and would meet him there. (These were the days of house calls.) We promised my parents we would call them immediately after the doctor's visit.

After he had examined Eileen, we asked his opinion as to whether we should leave Eileen and the children at home so Colleen and I could travel to Montreal to attend Bessy's funeral. He explained that flu and polio symptoms were almost identical, but he believed Eileen only had the flu. We could safely attend the funeral.

With much relief, we made arrangements for our trip to Montreal. We were to fly via an RCAF-scheduled flight to Ottawa, where we would be met by one of Colleen's relatives at Rockcliffe Airport to drive us to Montreal. My mother agreed to move into our quarters at Fort Osborne Barracks until our return. The children accepted our departure without fuss. As well, Eileen had already begun to show improvement.

The travel arrangements had so absorbed our attention that we had barely spent any time discussing Bessy's death until we were headed east.

In the austerity of a military aircraft, normally used for training para-troopers, it was a long, sad journey.

We deplaned at Rockcliffe and entered the terminal looking for Colleen's relatives. We heard the public address system request Major Donoghue to report to the desk. The message awaiting me there was that Eileen had been admitted to King George Isolation Hospital. She was suf-fering from polio.

My mother had noticed that Eileen could not swallow when she was sucking a lollipop. She called the army nurses. The polio had attacked her throat. The nurses obtained an ambulance and then arranged through Prairie Command to get the message to me at Rockcliffe.

When we arrived in Montreal, Colleen left immediately for the undertaker's to attend the wake while I began to arrange for our speedy return to Winnipeg. Our return was arranged with me travelling by RCAF and Colleen following later via TRANS CANADA Airlines (now Air Canada). Upon arriving in Winnipeg, I telephoned the doctor and learned that Eileen had not yet reached the crisis stage. It would still be a few more days before she did. As such, we were denied the right to see her. I had made the call from our quarters, which is on the airline's flight path, and heard Colleen's commercial flight pass overhead. She reached home an hour later.

Soon thereafter, our telephone began to ring. Our many friends had heard the news and were inquiring about Eileen's condition. Each time the phone rang, we were terrified it would be bad news about our daughter. We finally solved the problem by telling our closest friends, Ann and Mitchell Hanen, that we would inform them daily about Eileen's condition. In turn, they arranged a "fan-out" telephone system to all our other friends.

We and our army friends could follow Eileen's condition through the army nurses serving polio patients at King George Hospital. The army nurses' quarters were on the top floor of Building 22 in Fort Osborne bar-racks. Our apartment was on the floor below.

As nurses came off duty, one of them would call at our apartment and give us a progress report, demonstrating the close ties of the army commu-nity. The army is not only a community, it's a way of life. When serious problems arise, ranks close tightly. For several days, the nature of the reports were simply, "She's holding her own." Additional sources of infor-mation were our doctor and his son, both of whom visited Eileen regular-ly, and our pastor, who also kept a close eye on her condition.

The need for more nurses continued. Colonel C.G. Wood, command medical officer, drew on nurses from Greenwood, Nova Scotia; Esquimalt,

B.C.; and Churchill, Manitoba. In a mid-August interview with journalists, he pointed out that all of the armed forces were providing nurses. He had approached the medical policy board of the Department of National Defence, a new body designed to coordinate medical activities of the services, to supply nurses. Within less than a week, more nurses had arrived for duty. This group included 19 registered nurses and 18 medical assistants. Supplementing the large civilian nursing staff were nine army, four navy, and four RCAF nurses, as well as four navy and four medical assistants. Three of the nurses from Montreal's Military Hospital were on their way home from polio work in Whitehorse, Yukon, when they were ordered to report to Winnipeg. By mid-August, it was believed the incidence of cases had levelled off. Greater Winnipeg alone had 542 cases, but like the flood of 1950, the crest had not been reached. By 17 August the province reported 836 cases, 509 with paralysis. One week later, the toll was 1,055 cases, resulting in 25 deaths.

Despite the efforts of the medical community, the nurse shortage continued. The problem, though, was developing a different character. The need was no longer to meet the care required for a sudden influx of stricken patients. The King George Hospital staff needed more nurses and staff to handle the backlog of chronic and semi-chronic cases built-up during the epidemic.

In August, Dr. Elliott requested that I meet with him to discuss the nursing shortage and to render an opinion as to what might effect a solution. With Eileen in the isolation hospital, the staff shortage at the King George had been on my mind and I had been trying to determine a solution. The medical community and the provincial government had provided a constant flow of information about the epidemic to the public. They also had provided information designed to head off panic by pointing out that the large majority of patients would make a complete recovery. Dr. Elliott and others repeatedly reported on the shortage of nurses and staff and the newspapers and broadcasting stations publicized this regularly and accurately. I had not been involved in the preparation or transmission of this information.

The invitation from Dr. Elliott was probably the result of the PR task I had undertaken in the 1950 flood. Through that, I was acquainted with many members of the province's public service. Before meeting the deputy minister, I made a thorough review of the information which had been published. It resulted in a new viewpoint for me.

When I met with Dr. Elliott, I told him that I thought that the effects of the staff shortage on the nurses had not been fully reported. Although complete details of the number of cases, the nature of the disease, the possibility for recovery, and the shortage of nurses and support staff had been made available to the media (and subsequently passed along to the public), many people were still unaware what effect the nursing shortage was having. The information they were providing was important, but it was not the right message to recruit nurses.

My recommendation was that the media be invited to visit King George Hospital so that journalists could see for themselves the effects of the nursing shortage and then report the complete picture. I asked whether a party of journalists would be permitted to make such a visit.

The answer was yes, although the deputy minister pointed out that there was a small risk to those making the visit. I volunteered to extend an invitation to the newspapers, broadcasting stations, and wire services for their reactions. Dr. Elliott agreed.

I visited the various media outlets and, through the managers, extended the invitation, with the caution that there would be some risk involved for the journalists who chose to participate. Each newspaper and broadcasting station accepted. Before the visit was made, I warned each individual journalist that they were facing some risk. No one dropped out.

Medical staff conducted us through the wards where the numbers of patients needing constant care were overwhelming. There were also the tragic cases of those encased in iron lungs, which pumped steadily to keep the occupants' lungs drawing and expelling oxygen.

For me, however, the most shocking case was a tiny seven-year-old skeletal child standing in the corner of a large crib, clinging to the rails and staring at me in my uniform. Suddenly she began to cry, calling, "Daddy, daddy!"

It took me several seconds to realize that it was Eileen. As I moved towards her, a nurse stopped me and explained that I could go near her, but I was not allowed to touch her. I felt numb, as if I'd been hit in the stomach. I was almost sick.

I came within a few feet of Eileen and we spoke to each other. Moments later, I could barely recall what I had said. I do know that it took me a day or two to realize that she was not wearing the chest respirator originally given to her upon admission to the hospital. I took that to be an encouraging sign.

I later learned that the doctors decided against the iron lung and had used the chest respirator for only a short period. They relied primarily on Eileen to fight through to recovery. It was a good decision.

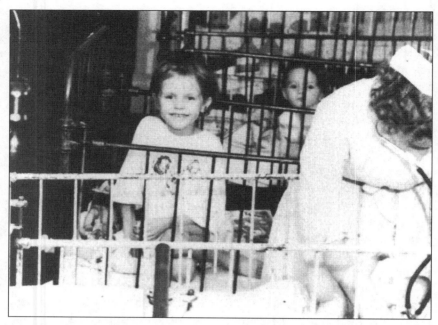

Eileen stopped crying when she saw photographer Paul Tomlin. Tomlin was sporting a six-inch-wide, wax-tipped moustache, of which he was justifiably proud. Sad to say, he had to shave it off when he was commissioned.
Courtesy Department of National Defence.

Sergeant Tomlin took a picture of Eileen standing in the crib in her hospital gown. As our youngest, Maureen, would say years later, "I have a 'ginger ale' nose each time I see that photo."

On Friday, 4 September the *Free Press* published an interview with Dr. John Gemmell of the Manitoba Medical College, who described the medical care being given to polio patients. Included was the following:

> Dr. Gemmell made a plea for more nurses and physiotherapists to assist in the present fight against polio. Many more are needed to care for the great number of new patients who are daily entering King George Hospital, he said.

This was the same type of appeal that had been broadcast and published regularly with very little effect. The Winnipeg media did not anticipate that journalists would be permitted to enter the isolation hospital to see for themselves the impact the staff shortages were having on the nurses.

The same day Dr. Gemmell's interview was published, I conducted the Winnipeg journalists through King George Hospital. What follows is excerpted from a story published by the *Winnipeg Free Press* after the visit. The *Winnipeg Tribune* and the broadcasting stations carried similar stories.

Small in Number, A 'Fighting' Few Stand Polio Siege

by Lyn Chandler

Statistics never tell the whole story.

Though [polio] case totals of more than 1,300 have broken all records ... another record has been broken that statistical records ignore.

It is a record of human endurance ... that belongs to a relatively small group of people in this city.

They are the people centred in the focal point of the province's polio attack – the King George Isolation Municipal Hospital.

From the laundry room to the office of the medical director, the work of the men and women at the hospital has been a matter of "slugging it out" – the consistent pressure of work piling up on them,– work that has been a matter of life and death. To most of them it's become routine to work a 12-to 14-hour day.

Caring for a respirator patient is one of the most arduous nursing jobs. The nurse is constantly on her feet working over the patient in a huge machine ... suctioning mucus from the nose and mouth, watching the pressure of the respirator and the oxygen, checking vital signs.

In some critical cases ... the nurse must work with her arms through small sponge rubber portholes in the side ... working in this position is an added physical strain.

... during the recent August heat wave, a nurse would come off duty from one of these wards with her uniform soaked with perspiration.

The hospital ... now has about 10 extra doctors and 10 additional junior interns. But the relief came in gradually.

Medical staffs from most city hospitals have pitched in ... volunteer[ing] three to four hours [each day]. Public Health nurses, army, air force and navy medical personnel and nurses from Veterans Affairs are [also] among the reinforcements.

... as the epidemic load lightens for the hospital, the rehabilitation work begins.

As the sound of the pulse of the iron lung carries through the hospital halls, so does the sound of the physiotherapists's voice saying, "Bend your knee, sweetie," as she gently nurses the stiffened limb of a child back to health.

The newspaper reports and broadcasts accomplished the purpose of the media tour. On Monday, large numbers of retired nurses volunteered their services after they had read and heard of the effects created by the shortage. In a few days, the problem was solved.

Few PR practitioners ever have the good fortune to work on a problem that is seriously affecting a member of his or her family. I have always been grateful that I was given such an opportunity.

Lessons I had learned in Muskox and Redramp were reinforced. As in those operations, a knowledgeable and competent spokesperson was made available to members of the media. Colonel Wood was essential to the achievement of the objective. He was a key military medical figure in providing information during the polio epidemic and the 1950 flood.

As always, accurate, adequate details must be provided – and in most cases this is best done by reporters. The stories that brought nurses back to duty were written by journalists who were given the opportunity to see and judge for themselves the conditions being created by the epidemic. News releases could never have achieved the same results.

The cooperation of operations individuals, such as Colonel Wood and Dr. Elliott, were essential. They were sympathetic to the reporters.

This story has another happy ending. Eileen recovered fully, and the little girl we almost lost grew up to earn her doctorate in psychology. (Thank you, Dr. Jonas Salk.)

Eileen Donoghue presents a bouquet to Madame Vanier, wife of Governor General Vanier (left), on their arrival at the Public Service Recreation Centre, Ottawa, to attend a fencing tournament.

CHAPTER 6

GERMANY

Put 6,000 Canadian soldiers in a foreign land in peacetime, add their wives and children, and the likelihood is that you'll quickly acquire a knowledge of community relations and other facets of the public relations function.

Differences in language, culture, and customs can result in misunderstandings and resentments between the local populace, the troops, and their families. In Germany, for example, trees are considered almost sacred. When you have a countryside exercise with tanks, the likelihood is some trees will be damaged. This is not the best way to foster good relations. One means of reducing problems is to seize opportunities that will help the two communities to know one another.

I had this experience twice. First, briefly with the 27th Canadian Infantry Brigade, and later with the 1st Canadian Infantry Brigade. The former, commanded by Brigadier Geoffrey Walsh, was the first Canadian formation to be posted abroad in peacetime. We went to Hanover, Germany, in 1951. I had been appointed to command the brigade's public relations unit.

Before going overseas, I accompanied Brigadier Walsh on a tour of the reinforcement companies stationed in Ontario and the Maritimes. During the tour, he and I had a disagreement. It took place at Fredericton, New Brunswick, where a news conference was scheduled in an officers' mess. He arrived a few minutes before me in a staff car. When I reached the mess, I went to the cloak room, then headed for the conference room. En route, I met the brigadier, who greeted me with, "Jack, I'll see the radio people first and then the newspaper reporters."

Stunned at this pronouncement and without stopping to think, I blurted out, "Sir, you can't do that!"

He retorted immediately. "Who the hell do you think is commanding this brigade?" He then spent the next two minutes from his towering height telling me exactly who was "The Boss" while I stood at attention.

When he ran out of steam, I said, "I'll do what you've ordered, but you must take responsibility for the results." I pointed out that the two categories of journalists were highly competitive. The radio journalists had the faster means of communication and both groups would be angry if two news conferences were held. From civilian experience, I knew two conferences on the same topic would present serious problems. All the questions from the two categories of journalists would not be the same. If a major point was raised by one conference and not the other, the one that had failed to ask the questions would feel they had been cheated.

Following a few seconds' silence, the brigadier said, "All right, have it your way." It was the beginning of a warm friendship.

Major Jack Donoghue leads the 27th Brigade Public Relations Unit aboard ship in Quebec City harbour for departure to Germany. Immediately behind the major is Lieutenant Mike Gausden, who in later years was employed in public relations by the Bank of Montreal and subsequently the Bankers' Association of Canada.

Courtesy Department of National Defence.

The Honourable Brooke Claxton, minister of national defence, speaks to news-
men in the Stadhius Chamber of Rotterdam before the inspection of the 27th
Brigade's guard of honour. Seated on the minister's right is Mr. Pierre Dupuy,
Canadian ambassador to the Netherlands.
Courtesy National Archives of Canada, PA 174265.

During the war, Walsh had earned a reputation as being one of the
Allies' best bridge builders when he was chief engineer of the First
Canadian Army. Later, he became a lieutenant-general, chief of the general staff (head of the army) at the same time I was director of public
relations (Army) at Defence Headquarters, Ottawa. Years later, I learned
he was familiar with the work of journalists. His father had been a well-
known newspaper editor in eastern Canada. I concluded that he may
have been wanting to learn if I was a "yes man," whose type he didn't
like.

Before leaving Canada, I requested a meeting with the Hon. Brooke
Claxton, minister of defence, something majors seldom do. I did not
expect the request to be granted, but it was. I was not clear about the
brigade's status and I knew European journalists would have questions
when we arrived. The government had announced that the brigade would
not be a part of the allied forces occupying Germany. It was to be
Canada's military commitment to the North Atlantic Treaty organization
(NATO).

Our meeting was brief and pleasant, but not entirely satisfactory. My main question was: "If the Canadian taxpayers are paying for the brigade's presence in Germany, who receives the money?" The cost of Allied occupation troops was being paid by the German public.

Claxton's response ended our discussion. "The only important fact," he replied, "is Canada is paying its own way and the presence of Canadian soldiers in Germany will not be a financial burden on the German people." I later learned that the cost of the Canadian NATO brigade was being paid to the Allied occupation authorities, not the Germans.

We landed in Rotterdam in November 1956. I was removed from the troop-ship by special launch at the request of the Canadian military attaché in The Hague.

At the Canadian Embassy, I was told I would be working with Gus Kies, a civilian and head of public relations in The Netherlands Defence Department. Our task was to prepare and execute the media relations aspects of a ceremonial parade in the square before the Stadhuis of Rotterdam 21 November, at which General Dwight D. Eisenhower, NATO Supreme Commander, would welcome the brigade to Europe.

Kies was knowledgeable and cooperative. In addition to the formal parade, we planned a news conference for Claxton which would follow the parade. A news kit was prepared, containing brief biographies of the participating dignitaries and a description of the brigade. The news conference was held in the Council Chamber of the Stadhuis, the most ornate surroundings I had ever, or would ever, see. In fact, halfway through the conference, Kies had uniformed waitresses serve tea, dainty sandwiches, and biscuits. Claxton outlined Canada's purpose in sending the brigade to Europe and responded to all questions.

The ceremonial parade had gone off without a hitch; but not so in the mind of Claxton. There were nearly 60 journalists covering the parade, almost one-half of them photographers and cameramen. The main objective of the parade was to let the world know that Canada had committed troops to NATO and that they were now in Europe.

The moment General Eisenhower appeared, took the salute, and started his inspection of the Guard of Honour, the photographers and cameramen swarmed like bees as they followed him. For two short months, just prior to the invasion of Normandy, I had served at Eisenhower's Supreme Headquarters. The sight of photographers and cameramen crowding around the general was not unusual nor disturbing to me. Not so for Claxton. Down came a messenger from the saluting base with a terse note from Claxton which read: "Stop those photographers."

General Dwight Eisenhower inspects the 58th Field Squadron, Royal Canadian
Engineers of the 27th Canadian Infantry Brigade on 21 November 1951. He is
accompanied by the officer commanding the squadron, Major R.W. Potts.
Courtesy National Archives of Canada, PA 174264.

Dignitaries chat at a Stadhius reception. Left to right: Brigadier Geoffrey
Walsh, brigade commander; a Netherlands government official; General
Eisenhower; the mayor of Rotterdam; and the Honourable Brooke Claxton,
minister of national defence.
Courtesy National Archives of Canada, PA 174263.

Despite the direct order, I had no intention of thwarting the parade's main objective, which could only be achieved by those photographers, cameramen, and reporters. I hustled around the photographers, stopping to hold one's elbow, and said, "How are you making out? Everything all right?" I then moved on to another. I received mostly puzzled looks, but I was certain that Claxton thought at least I was attempting to bring about some semblance of order.

At a reception held in the Stadhuis after the news conference, I was told that my former commander, Eisenhower, had saved my hide. A senior Canadian officer of the brigade said to me, "You're lucky. Claxton spoke to Eisenhower about the cameramen and how disruptive they had been. Eisenhower replied, 'You haven't seen anything yet. That was mild.'" Pictures of Eisenhower inspecting the Guard of Honour appeared in numerous European and North American newspapers, as well as in newsreels on both continents.

Soon after arriving in Hanover, I visited the Canadian Embassy in Bonn. I was introduced to British civilians from the Occupation Authorities and members of the German media, who were curious about the brigade's status. I gave them a short briefing on the brigade. They asked who Canada was paying for the presence of the brigade in Germany and I told them. I felt the occupation representatives were not too happy. I was glad I had confirmed the facts before the meeting. I was also pleased that I didn't receive a "rocket" from National Defence Headquarters in Ottawa through my brigadier.

My stay in Hanover with the 27th Brigade was short-lived. Colleen took seriously ill and, without asking Ottawa, Brigadier Walsh shipped me home. Because my stay was short, I had learned little about community relations.

First Brigade replaced the 27th Brigade and moved to Soest, Westfalia, the largest rural province in Germany. The 27th Brigade had established good community relations in the Hanover area, and it was the intention of Brigadier W.A.B. Anderson to do the same in Westfalia. Units of the brigade were based in Soest, Werl, and Iserlohn. This took place before I returned to Germany.

A few days after settling in, Brigadier Anderson prepared and extended invitations to the German media to attend a news conference to explain the brigade's community relations policies and methods of operation. It would also give the journalists an opportunity to question the brigadier.

Tragedy struck the night before the news conference when a Canadian soldier was apprehended and charged with murdering an elderly German woman. Should the news conference be cancelled or postponed? Captain Brian O'Regan, Acting Commanding Officer, advised the conference be held. Brigadier Anderson recognized quickly the common sense of this advice. Cancellation of the news conference would have proved disastrous. The media would have concluded that the brigadier was dodging the issue and would have reported as much. That would have aggravated the German public. In cases of unpleasant stories, a news conference is the best route to follow. It gives reporters the opportunity to question officials. It also helped that the head of the organization was an effective spokesperson.

I did not arrive in Germany until after the court-martial. Years later, I discussed the incident with (now General) Anderson. The German journalists were primarily interested in who would conduct the trial, the Canadian Army or German authorities. Anderson explained to them it would be a Canadian court-martial and that the German journalists would be permitted to cover the trial. When the life sentence was handed down, "opinion in the German press was that the sentence was too severe," Anderson told me. But as a result of the general's wise decision and the subsequent conduct of his troops, army community relations were back on track.

My introduction to 1st Brigade began with a unique community relations task. I was asked to return a 218-year-old Moroccan, leather-bound, handwritten book which had been "liberated" when a Canadian regiment captured the ancient town of Meppen.

After the war, the book had been given to Lieutenant-Colonel E.J.O. Granville, commanding officer of the Lake Superior Scottish Regiment in Port Arthur (now Thunder Bay). Granville sent the book back to Major-General N.E. Roger, general officer commanding, Prairie Command, headquartered at Fort Osborne Barracks, Winnipeg, where I was command public relations officer. At the time, I was preparing to leave for Germany. Thus I became the bearer of the purloined gift. I was not told, however, to whom in Meppen I should return the book .

It was several weeks after my arrival in Soest before I was able to visit Meppen. During that period, I became familiar with the brigade, my commander, and especially my interpreter, Herr. Erik Reichel. He had served as a senior non-commissioned officer with Field Marshal Erwin Rommel in the Africa Corps and had been taken prisoner and shipped to the United States, where his command of English improved.

It was my first experience in using an interpreter and I was uneasy. I wanted to assure myself that Reichel wouldn't soften interpretation of a critical German news story. I decided to test him. I obtained a story from the military police and Reichel translated it. His version was harsher than the original translation. As a result, I began training Reichel in the fundamentals of public relations. He proved an apt pupil and became even more valuable to the brigade.

The performance of the troops was the main factor in establishing and maintaining good community relations. Reichel was the next most important factor because through him we could speak to the German media and, hence, to the German population. It was clear to me that I had best get to know members of the seven daily newspapers in the communities of Soest, Werl, and Iserlohn. There were no broadcasting stations in the brigade area.

Once comfortable with the unit and the brigade, I set out with Reichel and the book for Meppen, which was a two-hour drive from Soest. En route, we decided to seek out the Bürgermeister (mayor) or the Oberkreistdirecktor (county director). We reached Meppen shortly before noon and after checking with the civic offices, we learned that the county director was attending a hotel luncheon, which we quickly located. In we marched. Reichel sent a hotel employee to the Oberkreistdirecktor with a request that he come to the lobby for a few minutes.

He arrived, a tall, slender, middle-aged man, looking somewhat puzzled. After Erik explained the purpose of our visit, I presented the leatherbound book to him. The county director examined it and broke into a broad smile, exclaiming, "Wunderbar! Wunderbar!" The book recounted the history of Meppen.

We had interrupted him during a meeting of the county's Cultural Society. He pressed us to join them for lunch, but we begged off, saying that we had to return immediately to the brigade.

Canadian troops had captured Meppen during the war, which made it almost a certainty that the residents would be interested in the story of the returned book. As a result, it was picked up by the media. It also appeared in other newspapers, including the newspapers in the brigade's area. The stories were favourable. Being NATO, and not occupation forces, contributed towards good community relations with the civilian population. Mine had been a much more pleasant introduction to the German authorities than the public relations officers had faced when the brigade first moved to Soest.

On returning from Meppen, I discussed with Reichel the question of getting to know the seven editors in the brigade area. I suggested that they probably had never been in a Canadian home and it might be best to meet them for the first time on my own ground. He agreed and prepared and delivered invitations for each editor and his wife to visit our married quarters in the evening for refreshments and a light lunch.

The editors arrived, but without their wives. Two editors spoke English. Conversations with the other five were translated by Reichel. The conversations gave me the opportunity to point out how pleased we would be to provide unclassified information about the brigade and its soldiers. I asked only that they consult us before publishing critical stories, giving us the chance to investigate and confirm the story they had, or whether it was misinformation. In short, I promised to tell them the truth. I pointed out that the brigade had provided them complete facilities to cover the court-martial trying the murder charge, indicating good faith and trust.

In the nearly two years I was in Germany, only once was a critical story not referred to me before publication. The Iserlohn newspaper reported that Canadian soldiers were driving automobiles that were not roadworthy. We had a few soldiers killed while driving cars they had purchased after arriving in Germany. German police and Canadian provost (the army police) investigated these accidents and provided the newspapers with the facts. The papers published this information. However, the Iserlohn newspaper, in a strongly worded editorial, stated that the brigade must take action and clean up the situation created by unworthy road vehicles. What the editor did not know was that German auto dealers were selling these cars to Canadian soldiers at ridiculously low prices. It was true that accidents had occurred. Through the provost, Brigadier Anderson learned about the situation. The provost was stopping Canadian soldiers driving personally owned cars and checking each vehicle's condition. If they were not found roadworthy, the car was impounded and the soldier told to arrange adequate repairs for the automobile before it could be released. Few did. This action had been taken several weeks before the Iserlohn editorial. Reichel translated a report of what the brigade had been doing and delivered it to the editor. The next day, the editor wrote an apology.

The only serious incident after the murder occurred more than a year later when I had taken over command of the public relations unit. The brigade had moved from Soest, Werl, and Iserlohn to Sennenlager, a German training area. At Sennenlager, we saw the segment of the supposedly impregnable French Maginot line of defence that the German army had reproduced. The Germans studied the Maginot line defence, replicated it, then developed a plan of attack against it, rehearsing it until it took on the features of a drill. As a result, their attack entirely destroyed the effectiveness of the Maginot line and most of France was overrun.

In the midst of the 1st Canadian Brigade's summer field training, a spate of critical stories appeared in the German press within the Sennenlager area that reported fighting between the troops and civilians in local beer parlours. I consulted Major John Dowsett, the brigade's provost marshal, who informed me there had been a few minor incidents, but nothing like what was described in the newspaper articles. Within 24 hours, the Canadian media had picked up the German stories and reported their content.

Sennenlager was outside the area of the brigade's home stations and I had had no contact with the media there. I decided that an effort should be made to have a Canadian journalist investigate the reported bad conduct of the troops. None that I knew were located in Germany. I telephoned the Southam Bureau located in London and explained the situation to Jack Stepler. He agreed to come to Sennenlager.

When he arrived, I assigned Reichel to assist him on a series of visits to German gasthauses (taverns) in the area. I decided not to accompany them, as I believed my uniform might influence the proprietors' responses.

They spent at least two days visiting the gasthauses. The proprietors were unanimous in their responses. They said the German newspaper articles were exaggerated and they had had little trouble with the Canadians. Stepler wrote his story for Southam and the incident dissolved in Canada. We also reported Stepler's findings to Major Dowsett. The German newspaper which had published the stories heard of Stepler's findings and demanded a meeting with German police authorities.

I attended the meeting with Dowsett and Reichel. The issue was debated warmly between journalists and the police. The debate revealed that the German police authorities wanted the Canadian Provost Corps to increase military patrols in the area. The German journalists concluded that the police had exaggerated accounts of friction with the troops to pressure Major Dowsett into increasing patrols. They later published this conclusion.

Every opportunity to involve the German populace in brigade events was seized. The municipal and county dignitaries would come to know the brigade and, if the event was large enough and facilities were adequate, the German public could be invited. They could judge for themselves the performance standards of the troops. I can recall three such events.

The first was a celebration of Canada Day held in Dortmund Stadium with units of the brigade competing in track-and-field events.

The commanding officer of the Princess Patricia's Canadian Light Infantry, Lieutenant-Colonel Stan Waters (who many may recognize as Canada's first elected Senator), added a western flair, obtaining inexpensive white stetsons for his troops and their families. The event was open to the German public.

The second occurred the year the Penticton V's won the world hockey title and then toured Germany. They played an exhibition game in Soest against an army team, attended by German authorities and residents of Soest. The captain of the V's presented an autographed hockey stick to the Bürgermeister. It ended up in the Soest museum next to some authentic letters written by Martin Luther.

I was privileged to inherit Captain Brian O'Regan as my second-in-command. At Brigadier Anderson's request, I loaned him to the Penticton V's to smooth their visit. He scrounged oxygen tanks from the Brits' medics for their games. Then he stirred the Canadian fans to shout "Go V's Go!", which is in use today in a variety of forms. Andy O'Brien, a Montreal sports columnist, credited Brian with the creation of the cry.

The third event involved a Canadian youth choir, for whom the Canadian Embassy in Bonn was looking for engagements. The brigade arranged a concert in the Soest auditorium. Reichel translated into German introductory remarks for General Anderson. Anderson worked hard rehearsing the introduction and startled the audience with a presentation in their own language. The choir played to a packed house and the newspaper reviews of the concert were all deservedly complimentary. The Canadian youths were a hit.

Reichel translated for me all the stories published about Canadians in the seven German newspapers. I had each story placed in one of three categories: favourable, unfavourable, and neutral; as well, I recorded the length of each column in inches. The statistics were compiled monthly for each category. It was a crude method, but it did provide a measure of the quantity and quality of the information about Canadians reaching the German public. The results showed favourable stories heavily outnumbering the other two categories. After about three months, O'Regan and I suggested to Reichel that German readers might be becoming tired of reading about Canadians and that he might pass along that hint to the editors. The coverage, however, didn't drop significantly.

Information to the Canadian public wasn't neglected. Members of the unit produced "hometowner" stories and pictures about the soldiers' activities and those of their families. Major stories and photographs of events such as military exercises were produced by visiting Canadian and foreign correspondents. While visiting the brigade, these correspondents were provided with accommodation and meals. When visiting units to witness events and obtain briefings and interviews, they were accompanied by a PR conducting officer. All of these arrangements were made through the PR unit.

The visit of Douglas Lachance of the Canadian Broadcasting Corporation's (CBC) national radio network based in Paris is one example. Lachance wrote me before Christmas; he wanted to produce a radio network feature on the brigade and the families for broadcast during the festive season. We made arrangements for him to obtain interviews with the soldiers while visiting individual units. He also interviewed unit chaplains and family members.

We were anxious to provide material about the brigade's German environment. This was accomplished by arranging for the choir of Soest's thousand-year-old cathedral to sing carols and Christmas hymns in the choir loft while Lachance recorded them.

He wrote me after Christmas to say that CBC Toronto was pleased with the production.

The brigade's community relations efforts and the flow of information to the German people contributed to the maintenance of a good rapport with the public. Two factors not planned – nor recommended – by the public relations unit made major contributions to stable relations. Anderson insisted on good behaviour of his troops and he was meticulous in the relations with German authorities. He carried on the high standard set by Walsh's 27th Brigade. The second factor was the number of Canadian army families that took the decision to live in rented German accommodations. A significant number of families took this route while married quarters were under construction. While many moved into the married quarters when construction was completed, the families that continued to live in the German homes and apartments earned a positive reputation with their neighbours.

The quality of relations with clients, media, and general and special publics depends in great measure on their perception of your integrity and that of the organization employing you. The reasons a high standard of community relations were achieved were numerous. Among them were:

1. On the arrival of Canadian soldiers in Europe in 1951, it was emphasized they had come to contribute to the defence of western Europe, under the North Atlantic Treaty Organization (NATO), and would be based in Germany. They were not occupation troops. This message

was repeated when the soldiers arrived in the Hanover area and again in 1953 when the brigade moved to the Soest area.

2. News releases and photos released to the German media referred to the soldiers as NATO troops. These releases kept the civilian populace informed of the soldiers' and their families' activities.

3. The brigade commanders stressed with their officers the importance of maintaining good community relations. In turn, the officers transmitted this message to the troops.

General Alfred Gruenther (left), NATO supreme commander, paid a farewell visit to the 1st Canadian Infantry Brigade before turning over his command to become head of the American Red Cross. On his arrival he was greeted with a guard of honour and a scroll recognizing the fact that he had served longer in the rank of second lieutenant than anyone else in the American army. It was presented by Lieutenant Willie Schuller, who belonged to the Princess Patricia's Canadian Light Infantry and was president of the Society for Prevention of Cruelty to Subalterns. Gruenther had been Eisenhower's chief of staff during the war. At right, the author; centre, W.A.B. Anderson.
North Atlantic Treaty Organization photo.

4. On appropriate occasions, local dignitaries were invited to military social events and, when sporting events and facilities permitted, the general public was invited.
5. Prompt action was taken on complaints.

The arrival of Canadian troops in Germany in 1951 was the first occasion our soldiers were sent abroad in peacetime to contribute to defence operations. The performance of the officers and men resulted in praise from European military and civilian authorities, among them General Alfred Gruenther, NATO Supreme Commander.

In November 1956, Canadian troops formed the nucleus of the first-ever United Nations Emergency Force when they took up positions in the Gaza Strip. Since then, members of the Canadian Armed Forces have served in more than 30 different operations in foreign lands, ranging from truce observance to the supervision of elections.

During the period 1947–93, between 80,000 and 90,000 members of the Canadian Armed Forces have served on peacekeeping missions in foreign countries. This high figure includes participation in the Korean police action. A precise figure is unobtainable because some individuals have carried out as many as five different peacekeeping assignments.

CHAPTER 7

NIGERIA

The Nigerian Civil War (1967–70) saw the great powers split. Britain, the Soviet Union, most Western countries, and the countries of Africa and the Third World supported the Nigerian Government. France and the Scandinavian countries supported the Ibo natives who wanted independence. Some Western missionaries with churches in Biafra, home of the Ibos, also supported the independence movement. There were suggestions in the international community that Nigeria's natural resources were the major powers' interests.

Public relations played a role on both sides of the war. Charges of genocide against the Ibos were appearing more frequently in the world press. A Swiss public relations firm had been retained to tell the Ibos' story and raise money for the cause. The objective was to keep the Ibos fighting for independence and arouse world opinion to pressure the Nigerian government.

In a formal invitation on 6 September 1968, the federal military government of Nigeria, realizing it was losing the war in the international media, requested Canada, Poland, Sweden, the United Kingdom, the Organization of African Unity, and the United Nations to send observers to inspect the federal military operations in the war-affected zones.

Ottawa accepted the invitation and designated a former director of Canadian Army public relations to be the senior Canadian on the observer team: Major General W.A. (Bill) Milroy, to whom I had been deputy director.

I first came into contact with Milroy in 1956 when he was responsible for army operations and training in Maritime Command, with headquarters in Halifax. I was at the Canadian Army Staff College in Kingston,

Lieutenant-General W.A. Milroy, wearing the uniform of colonel of the regiment of the Lord Strathcona's Horse (RC), when he visited the unit in Calgary to attend a change-of-command ceremony. Looking on is the author. Milroy solved the major PR problem in the Nigerian Civil War.
Canadian Forces Base Calgary photo.

Ontario, when the students were assigned to act as umpires during the large-scale summer military exercises at Camp Gagetown, New Brunswick. As general staff officer, Grade I, Milroy played a major role in the planning and operation of the summer exercises. I saw him at a briefing in which he participated, but only fleetingly during the exercise. He was of average height, about five feet, eleven inches, with a fair complexion. He had a pleasant personality. We didn't get to know one another that summer.

However, the following fall, when I was serving in Ottawa as deputy director public relations (Army) after graduation from the staff college, word arrived that Lieutenant-Colonel Milroy would succeed the retiring director, Lieutenant-Colonel Hector Stewart. As deputy director, I was responsible for preparing the hand-over documents and arranging a brief ceremony for the signing. I'd not heard that Milroy had been a journalist or had any background in public relations. I wondered what manner of director we were acquiring. I soon learned.

The signing took place in the director's office. Afterward, I returned to my desk just outside the director's door and left the two to chat. Shortly afterward, Milroy escorted Stewart to the door and they said their farewells.

Returning to his office as he passed my desk, Milroy said, "Come in, Jack, I'd like to have a talk with you."

He came to the point immediately. "You know how much I know about public relations," he said. "Until I tell you differently, I want you to teach me PR." It was the beginning of a long and lasting friendship.

Only after we had both retired from the army did I ask Milroy if he was surprised by his appointment and whether at that point he thought his military career had come to a dead end. "There was no question that the appointment was totally unexpected," he explained. "When the chief of staff of Eastern command phoned on a Saturday morning to tell me, I replied: 'What did you say?' He answered: 'You heard me correctly.' However, once I had taken the PR course and taken over – in fact even before that – it was obvious the appointment would be a challenging and interesting one." Before the changeover, he attended a 10-week PR course at Fort Slocum, New York.

Milroy's appointment had been made by Brigadier Fred Clift, the director general of staff appointments in Ottawa. Previously, Clift had been chief of staff at Prairie Command Headquarters, Winnipeg, when I was the command's public relations officer. Clift had acquired a sound knowledge of the PR function and recognized the principle that "PR is a command responsibility." In civilian terms, line officers have a PR responsibility that is not confined to the director of PR and the PR staff. Also, Milroy's appointment provided a potential senior commander an opportunity to gain knowledge of the public relations functions.

Milroy's appointment was important to me. A PR staff officer not only can assist an operations officer in learning PR principles and activities, he can acquire a more detailed knowledge of operations which will contribute to a greater appreciation of operations policies, plans, and programs. As we came to know one another, he taught me more than I taught him. He had fought in Italy and northwestern Europe as a squadron commander, and after the war, had become a superb staff officer. I had just graduated from the army's staff college and was struggling to apply to the PR function the knowledge I had gained. While I imparted PR principles, Milroy assigned me a constant stream of position papers.

As each paper was completed, it became a chapter in a manual of instructions: detailed instructions for PR operations at army headquarters, Ottawa; the commands across Canada; the PR detachments overseas; the militia PROs across Canada; the training of photographers; PR operations in an active theatre; Department of National Defence Photo Production Section of DPR (Army); the PRO at Royal Military College, Kingston, Ontario; and PR in a national survival operation. These instructions set forth the procedures governing normal PR operations in Ottawa, across Canada, and overseas. They covered responsibilities, planning, lines of communication, passage of information, information on publicity received, responsibilities of the individual appointments, processing releases, distribution of releases (including mailing lists), queries, type of releases, and many other details. I saw a lot of red ink.

Within a year, the directorate had undergone an extensive overhaul. Milroy was highly respected in the upper echelons of national defence and the directorate benefitted. He convinced the adjutant-general that highly competent officers from the combat corps should serve two years in public relations. These postings were carried out in the command headquarters that stretch from coast to coast in Canada.

Two infantry majors were the first to be posted and one, if not both of them, thought his military career had gone down the tube. But when they completed their two-year posting, each was promoted to lieutenant-colonel and given an infantry battalion to command – the dream of all infantry officers! The directorate received a flood of applications from all corps to serve two years with PR.

The armed forces have continued to train officers in the PR function. Their ability to effectively brief the media was demonstrated during the Oka incidents, the Gulf War, and the conflict in the former Yugoslav republic.

The War

Looked upon by other countries as a working democracy, Nigeria was split internally by tribalism. It had at least 200 tribes with different languages and a variety of cultures and religions. The estimated population of the three major groups was 13 million Ibos in the east, nine million Yoruba in the west, and the largest group, 24 million Fulani-Hausa in the north. The educated Yoruba and Hausa tended to be lawyers, doctors, and teachers. The educated Ibos included those in the professions, but they also had entered mechanics trades and management.

The civil war the observer team was flying into lasted more than three years, ending in 1970. The conflict began as an army coup by six officers of the Ibo tribe who murdered the federal prime minister in Lagos. But they failed to eliminate the head of the army, Major-General John Aguiyi-Ironsi. And although army officers in two of the other three regions of the country succeeded in killing the civilian head of the regions, Major-General Agiuyi-Ironsi, himself an Ibo, snuffed out the coup and endeavoured to concentrate power in Lagos.

Ironsi's attempts inflamed the tribes of the regions and the army factions. Northern soldiers came into conflict with Ibo soldiers in the south. Ironsi was murdered by his own soldiers, who believed he had been trying to take over the whole of Nigeria for the Ibo tribe.

The appointment of Ironsi's successor sowed the seeds for the civil war. Lieutenant-Colonel Yakubu Gowan, a practising Christian, was appointed and shortly after promoted to major-general. The military governor of the eastern region, Colonel Ojukwu, was more senior and resented the appointment. Atrocities against the Ibos had been committed and in at least one instance more than 100 had been slain. Ojukwu exaggerated the charges and the belief was generated that the Ibos faced genocide. The rivalry resulted in the outbreak of fighting with Ojukwu commanding the secessionist forces of Biafra, and Gowan the forces of the federal military government of Nigeria.

Milroy's briefings at External Affairs stressed retaining independence of the team's action. Then on his flight to London, in September 1968, he reviewed the situation as he knew it and concluded that the war was being fought through the news media. He realized that to be effective, the observers would have to involve the media in their operations. In this way, the team would not be the target of news reports. If the team's reports were accurate, they would be supported by the media.

The invitation authorized the team representatives of Canada, Britain, Sweden, and Poland to produce a report that would be sent to their countries. The team proposed the reports be released to the media 24 hours later at a Lagos news conference. The Nigerian military government adopted a hands-off policy and did not participate in these conferences.

In the initial briefing General Gowan, for the first time, requested that information copies of the team's reports be provided to his government. This requested change to the original invitation opened the way for the team to request its own changes, one of which was that media representatives be permitted to accompany the team. The request was granted.

The granting of this request achieved credibility and acceptance for the observer team's reports. The international team reported that the area on which it concentrated was about 70 miles deep and 50 miles wide; but they were able to go into the war-affected region where and when they wanted.

The team began its inspection in the First Division area based at Enugu, the eastern region's capital. There, the team split into two groups and straws were drawn to see who would head each group. Milroy drew the trip south and the senior British observer the east.

Accompanying the team were 15 journalists, eight Nigerians and seven foreign media representatives. The original intention was also to split the journalists into two groups. But word was received that a dissident airfield in the south had been captured. All the journalists opted for the trip south with Milroy.

Milroy reported that the group reached a brigade headquarters about 2:00 p.m. The road to the airfield was a raised track through low ground covered with very high grass. Fighting had been reported there in the morning. The track was blown at a culvert. An Indian photographer for *Time* and *Life* magazines had been killed earlier in an ambush.

After consideration Milroy decided to press on. Through the brigade headquarters, he arranged for transport to come back to the break in the road, a distance of about three to four miles. When the four observers and 15 journalists arrived at the break, stretcher bearers were crossing it with wounded soldiers.

After a brief delay, the group arrived at the "airfield," which comprised a mobile control vehicle and an undulating piece of highway which had been used as a landing strip.

The journalists sifted through papers in an improvised hut from which the airfield had been controlled. The next problem for the seven foreign journalists was to get their stories out. Milroy arranged their transport back to Enugu where they managed to get aboard a Red Cross aircraft for the flight back to Lagos where they could file their stories.

Later, the head of the BBC-TV team, on behalf of all the journalists, expressed thanks for the cooperation they had received from Milroy. Milroy generally believed that when permission was given for journalists to accompany the observers, the Nigerian military government viewed them as members of the team and were therefore entitled to the same treatment. Hence, they could not be hassled or forbidden to go anywhere where the observers went. In contrast, journalists who tried to go on their own were given short shrift and sent back to Lagos.

Major-General W.A. Milroy (left) and Major-General Arthur Rabb, senior Swedish observer, on a ferry in the Cross River area of Nigeria. The arm band reads "O.T.N., Observer Team to Nigeria."

Major-General W.A. Milroy (right), senior Canadian member of the International Observers Team in Nigeria, with a 1st Infantry Division warrant officer and his young local interpreter. "The Division had overrun the area occupied by the Ibos. The Warrant Officer spoke no Ibo, the youngster's language was Ibo and he also spoke the Warrant Officer's language and surprisingly good English. We visited the market place to check on local conditions just after the journalists had left the 'airfield' for Lagos."
Courtesy Lieutenant-General W.A. Milroy.

During the inspection trips, the team checked on the existence of a code of conduct for federal government troops; existence of medical, feeding, and rehabilitation facilities for displaced persons; presence of Ibos in government, the armed forces and commerce in territory held by the federal military government; and whether abandoned Ibo property was being protected.

The stops at camps and villages were impromptu and, whenever a team member wished, people on the highway would be stopped and questioned. The team found occupied villages where there were no signs of warfare or damage. They witnessed large numbers of refugees who had come out of the dense bush where they had been hiding. They were being fed and assisted by the Red Cross workers. Signs of malnutrition among children were seen, but they were being treated by doctors. Medical stores were in short supply, but the problem was believed to be one of transport.

In the Third Marine Commando Division, the team interviewed Red Cross officials looking after 200,000 refugees living together with the civilian administration and the army. In the Second Division, the team visited a camp run by Ibos and inhabited by 1,000 members of the tribe.

Questioned about the scarcity of educated Ibos in the federal troops area, Milroy reported there were not many in the northern and southern areas. The team believed they had retreated with the Biafran troops.

"In the mid-western state," Milroy reported, "the towns are operating and the schools are all going. They are not operating in the First and Third Division areas. Two of the members of the Governor's Council of the mid-western state are Ibos. There are Ibos in the civil service; the teachers are going there. So, the educated Ibos are back in the mid-western state, but in the east-central state, we think that probably they are really the ones who are withdrawing with the Ibos' forces." He added they saw no evidence of educated Ibos being persecuted.

Two criticisms of the observing team were that they had not visited secessionist territory and should have investigated atrocities as distinct from genocide. The team's response was that it could not concern itself with past atrocities that had taken place in the previous year and a half. The team focus was on what was currently taking place and hopefully the team's presence would deter atrocities.

Milroy also said the team was prepared to investigate complaints of current atrocities if these were received. He said the team already had been trying to investigate an alleged atrocity reported by Canadian sources. But the information they received was inadequate and they had been unable to locate the village named.

Reliable sources had reported people were starving behind the Biafran lines. This was known. And atrocities by Biafran troops against Ibos was highly unlikely.

The question before the team took the field was: Will our report be believed? Milroy's PR experience helped bring about a solution that he described in his testimony. Before implementing the solution, the team had explained its necessity to the federal military government and obtained agreement.

Milroy appeared before the parliamentary Standing Committee on External Affairs and National Defence on 22 and 23 October. Dennis Foley of the *Ottawa Citizen* covering the hearing reported:

> Members of the Commons external affairs committee persistently pricked away at Major General William Milroy for nearly five hours, with three conclusions emerging patently clear:

> - No one was going to trip up the 48-year-old general.
> - The International Inspection Team had uncovered no factual evidence of genocide.
> - The inspection team had gone about its work in a manner that no one could fault it for being led around by the nose.

Foley also commented that the general remained pleasant and forthright throughout – even when answering the same question for the fifth or sixth time.

The appointment of the observer team reversed the tide of the international media's coverage. Journalists judged the team's reports credible, and so reported.

Milroy returned to Nigeria and served there from September 1968 to the end of January 1969. That same year he set up the Canadian Defence Education Establishment in Ottawa, a command incorporating the National Defence College, the Armed Forces staff colleges, the staff school, and three military colleges. In 1971, he took over Training Command. When he retired in 1975 with the rank of lieutenant-general, he was responsible for the recruiting, training, education, and career management of military and civilian people in the Department of National Defence. Those who served with him were pleased, but not surprised.

The presence of the media with the observer team was key. Had the reporters not been present, the likelihood is that the observer team would have been discredited. Official acceptance by Nigeria of the media gave the reporters the same administrative status as the observers. They were provided with briefings, transportation, and accommodation. They were treated equally and there were no favourites. Releasing the reports 24 hours after they were dispatched to the government ensured the freshness of the stories generated by the Lagos correspondents. They were not "scooped" by journalists in the capitals of Canada, the United Kingdom, Sweden, and Poland.

The method of release, a news conference, contributed to the credibility of the observer teams and their reports. The reporters could question the team's spokesman about all aspects of the reports.

Finally, Milroy, before the parliamentary committee, displayed all the necessary skills of a spokesperson to discuss and transmit knowledge on the issue to committee members and through the reporters to the Canadian and international public.

CHAPTER 8

PR AND ROYALTY

Many titles have sprung up over the years to describe the public relations function. The one I like least is "public affairs." Too many affairs today are made public, as the Royal family could well attest. During my career I have had the good fortune of contributing to Royal visits while in the army and the public and the private sectors. I have already described my first brush.

My second involved PR planning when the Duke of Edinburgh visited 1st Canadian Infantry Brigade in Soest, Westfalia, Germany, to present the Royal Canadian Regiment (RCR) with their colour in 1954. Before Philip's arrival, I met with Lieutenant-Colonel Gordon E. Corbould, commanding officer of the RCR, Canada's oldest regiment. I encountered several difficulties. For one, Corbould insisted there would be no photographers on the parade square. They could use only telephoto lenses.

The sanctity of the parade square was demonstrated shortly after the war at Currie Barracks, Calgary, Alberta, home of the Princess Patricia's Canadian Light Infantry (PPCLI). There were many more married officers and men on the base than before the war. The storied regimental sergeant-major's (RSM) office looked out on the parade square. A young mother taking her infant for a stroll started across the square. The window slammed open. The dreaded RSM in his best parade-square voice demanded, "Madame, get that vehicle off my parade square."

I withdrew from the meeting with Corbould and let the matter rest for a few days. I reopened the issue with a note to Corbould, recommending that Sergeant Al King, a photographer with my No. 1 Public Relations Unit, and myself be permitted to move onto the square to get a close-up shot when Philip made the presentation. The civilian news photographers could be guided to suitable locations from which satisfactory photos could be obtained during the remainder of the ceremony. Sgt. King's photo could be developed and printed at the PR unit and prints made available to the visiting photographers at the conclusion of the ceremony. Corbould agreed.

The PR unit then began preparation of an information kit for the media while I sought and obtained the cooperation of Soest commercial photo establishments to permit use of their darkroom facilities by the visiting news photographers.

The plan progressed smoothly, but I continued to nurse a serious concern. During a visit Philip made with his children to Gibraltar, they were constantly subjected to the scrutiny of photographers. While the children were feeding Gibraltar's legendary apes, Philip tossed some of the feed towards the photographers. The incident was reported in the British press and for a period of time – until Philip apologized – his image was deleted from news photos of royal events. I was wondering how he would react to the presence of Sgt. King and myself on the parade square during the ceremony's most significant moment.

The day of the event, the RCR were drawn up on the square, while the dignitaries, reporters, cameramen, photographers, and members of my unit were gathered around the square awaiting the Duke's arrival. He arrived by helicopter on time, to the minute. But the instant he stepped out of the aircraft, a cloudburst soaked him and everyone present. Dripping wet, he mounted the saluting base and the ceremony began while my apprehensions mounted.

He marched out onto the square when the time arrived to present the colour. King and I followed slightly to the side and behind him. When he halted, we took up our position a few feet from him. As we did, without moving his head, he looked out of the corner of his eye and saw us. I held my breath. Then he looked straight ahead. Not a word was said. King obtained his picture, exposing only one frame, and we marched smartly off the square. King jumped into a jeep and sped off to the unit darkroom to produce the prints.

The picture was excellent and the media was pleased. Philip, despite the discomfort of the rain, was pleasant to all throughout the ceremony and afterwards. He was especially friendly when chatting with the officers and men after the formalities ended.

I met the Duke again in May 1960 under much less formal circumstances. Members of the Canadian War Correspondents' Association (CWCA), of which I am a member, visited London, England, to host a dinner at the Cafe Royale for members of the London Press Club who, during the war, had made the club's facilities available to Canadian correspondents. Charles Lynch, a Southam newspaper columnist, was president of the association. Arrangements also were made for Canada's barbershop quartet, The Nighthawks of London, Ontario, to accompany us. Philip had accepted an invitation to be guest speaker.

Trans-Canada Airlines made available a DC-8 jet for the flight. The flight on 27 May 1960 was officially timed and a new record of five hours and 44 minutes and 42 seconds was set for the Atlantic crossing. An official inaugural flight for the DC-8 came later.

Field Marshal Alexander had declined an invitation to the black tie dinner for health reasons. But when we landed at Heathrow Airport and taxied to the ramp, Lynch spotted Alexander on the tarmac. The former governor-general of Canada had come to welcome us. Charlie quickly hustled the barbershop quartet to the aircraft door. When it opened they stepped out onto the platform atop the steep set of stairs. We came down the steps to the tune of "Alexander's Ragtime Band" to receive a brief but warm welcome from a man we all admired.

The Nighthawks, who had entertained us during dinner, along with a small group of correspondents and the Prince gathered around the piano after dinner for a singsong. Philip was an enthusiastic participant. Finally, he excused himself, saying the hour was late and he had better be getting home. And off to Buckingham Palace he went.

Five years later, in 1959, Her Majesty and Prince Philip visited Canada. Queen Elizabeth presented colours to four regiments while Philip visited the RCRs in London, Ontario.

Queen Elizabeth's first presentation was to the Royal 22nd Regiment (the Van Doos) at a ceremonial parade on the Plains of Abraham. We had correctly anticipated a large turnout of journalists, photographers, and cameramen not only from across Canada but also the United States. *Life* magazine's outstanding photographic essayist Alfred Eisenstaedt was among those accredited.

In the intervening five years I had refined the method of working with the media photographers and cameramen during military ceremonies.

The objective of the new method was to provide the media with the best positions to obtain suitable photos and to guide them from one position to another without interfering with the ceremony. This would result in a high-quality photo record of the events and an extensive presentation of them to the North American public.

The principle on which the method was based was simple. The first factor was the source and direction of the light essential for producing satisfactory photos. In short, what will be the position of the sun relative to the ceremony? The ideal conditions occur between 10 a.m. and 2 p.m. The army's ceremonial manual is the bible which dictates every position and movement of the troops and the central dignitary. The best position is to have the troops left flank at right angles to the sun. This provides effective side lighting for the troops and the dignitary, in this case the Queen. And during the march past, the troops would be facing the sun and the Queen would be side lighted.

The next factor to consider was the distance between the Queen taking the salute and the soldiers closest to her in the march past. The ideal distance is 10 to 15 feet. If more than 20 feet, it would be almost impossible to catch the Queen taking the salute and the troops in the same frame.

At rehearsals, routes to and from the positions were selected that not only would not interfere with the troops but also would not make it necessary for the photographers to run from one point to the next.

Elevated positions for "live" television are essential to prevent the photographers from interfering with the cameramen. Sometimes compromise is necessary, and the reasons for this is explained in the briefing of the media, which usually takes place the day before Royal visits.

Dress rehearsals provide an opportunity not only to solve the photo problems on the ground but also to obtain close-up photos and film sequences that cannot be recorded the day of the event. Two army officers act as guides to move the photographers from position to position and two RCMP constables prevent unauthorized amateur photographers from joining the official, accredited photographers. The antics of the unauthorized photographers can cause trouble. The spectators can't distinguish the two categories and, invariably, the professionals are blamed for disrupting the ceremony.

The RCMP constables move in the rear of the group and assist in keeping it compact as they move to the designated positions.

The rehearsal on Parliament Hill unearthed a problem. If the directives of the ceremonial manual were properly adhered to, the Queen would have been screened at the ceremony's crucial moment, when she presented the Colour (see photos). Immediately after the rehearsal, we held a meeting of a few of the most senior army officers at Defence Headquarters and the decision was taken to reverse the manual's directions.

On the left, the rehearsal for Queen Elizabeth's presentation of colours on Parliament Hill; on the right, the presentation itself.
Courtesy Department of National Defence.

The Van Doos' ceremony on the Plains of Abraham was unique and done with the élan for which the regiment is famous. They buried microphones in the ground along a line on which the regiment would halt following the Advance in Review Order, the final movement of the ceremony. They kept the plan secret. This was not difficult, as the microphones were not visible.

When the final movement was completed, the bandmaster left his band behind the troops, marched out front, turned and faced the troops, and raised his baton. When he brought it down, the band and the troops broke into "God Save The Queen." They sang in French.

I was standing with the photographers within 15 feet of the Queen. She was wearing a canary yellow dress and hat to match. Shortly after the hymn began, she quietly slipped a handkerchief from her sleeve and for an instant touched it to her face. The photographers missed it. She had wiped a tear away.

The media cooperated in all of the presentations. Excellent coverage was obtained, including an extensive photo essay by Eisenstaedt in the 6 July 1959 edition of *Life* magazine. He was kind enough to write us later

Crowds lined up for two blocks in front of Canada's Geological Survey Building, waiting to see the moon soil samples. More than 25,000 people visited the exhibit during the four days the samples were on display.
Courtesy Department of Energy, Mines and Resources.

Deputy Minister Claude Isbister (far right) of Energy, Mines and Resources and members of the department view the plastic globe-encased moon soil samples.
Courtesy Department of Energy, Mines and Resources.

to say that we had provided the best opportunities to photograph royalty he had ever experienced. He added that he had been permitted to photograph the Queen from positions closer than on any previous occasion.

Near the conclusion of the Quebec City event, the media representatives and myself were invited to an evening reception aboard the *Britannia*, docked in Wolf's Cove. Each of us was greeted by Her Majesty and Prince Philip as we stepped from the gangplank to the deck. It was the first time I had spoken to Her Majesty. It was brief, a "Good evening and welcome aboard."

The reception took place on the fantail where the Royal couple moved separately among the guests, stopping at each group to chat. All of the journalists and photographers enjoyed the event and among the most enthusiastic were the Americans.

I met Prince Philip after I retired from the army in 1965 and was director of public relations and information services with the Department of Energy, Mines and Resources. In 1969, the department's Geological Survey of Canada was provided with samples of the first material returned to earth from the moon landing during the U.S. National Aeronautics and Space Administration's (NASA) *Apollo II* mission. Three years earlier, NASA had asked the Geological Survey to submit a study program for the moon material. The following year, a five-part study plan was submitted. NASA accepted all five proposals from among 400 submitted from around the world. One hundred and forty-two principal investigators were to receive samples, 32 of them scientists outside the USA. The reputation of Canada's Geological Survey was attested by the fact that five scientists of the Survey were chosen, along with a sixth Canadian, Dr. D.W. Strangway, Department of Geophysics, University of Toronto, to study the moon samples.

The studies covered petrological and mineralogical properties; magnetic properties; electrical conductivity; elemental concentrations and isotopic abundance rations; and chemical analysis.

PR implications mounted when NASA authorized public display of the moon samples for two days. NASA provided panels containing the story and photos of *Appollo II*. I conceived the idea of setting these up in the form of a corridor through which the public would pass slowly until reaching a room whose ceiling, floor, and walls were entirely black. The sole lighting was three pinpoint spotlights in the ceiling directed on the three samples, each in claws on the top of a rod centered in a plastic globe. It worked. The samples glowed just like the moon. The public read the story and viewed the photos as they moved towards the blacked-out room.

Prince Philip arrives with the Honourable Joe Green (right),
minister of Energy, Mines and Resources, to view the moon rocks.
The author is walking behind the minister.
Courtesy Department of Energy, Mines and Resources.

Deputy Minister Isbister (left), Prince Philip, and Minister of Energy, Mines and
Resources Joe Green examine Canadian rock samples.
Courtesy Department of Energy, Mines and Resources.

There, they walked up a slightly raised platform, looked on the spotlighted globe and samples, and then left the building.

The public proved just as excited to view the samples as the scientists. Thousands attended the two-day exhibit and many had to be turned away. As a result, a second two-day exhibit was authorized by NASA and more than 25,000 citizens viewed the moon samples by the end of the four days.

I left the building late in the evening on the last day of the exhibit. As I stepped through the doorway, a brilliant full moon appeared high in the sky. Within yards behind me were the three pieces of the moon. I stood for several minutes overwhelmed at the accomplishments of *Apollo II.*

Prince Philip, visiting Canada at that time, expressed a wish to see the exhibit. He spent a half hour examining the samples and questioning the five principal investigators. I spoke to him briefly and he asked if the public had turned out in large numbers to see the exhibition, which he thought was splendid. It was the first time I had met him as a civilian. (I met him again twice briefly when a society he sponsored held meetings in Calgary. I was then vice-president of FWJ and my involvement was confined to media relations.)

I was to meet Her Majesty once more, in June 1990, when she visited Red Deer and Calgary, Alberta. My involvement began when the Queen expressed a wish to visit the Red Deer General Hospital to see its unique pediatric unit. I had been the FWJ consultant to the hospital before the new state-of-the-art building opened in 1980. The pediatric unit opened in February 1990. Working with Roger Walker, vice-president, whose responsibilities included PR, we produced and received palace approval of a plan for the visit.

The façade of patients' rooms reflected business firms and services seen in a town, such as the fire department, bank, and City Hall. The rooms faced a central children's play area where nurses were stationed to supervise the children, while monitoring patients in their rooms on closed-circuit TV.

Coverage of the event was national and international, resulting in hospital representatives from Canada and the United States visiting Red Deer to study the pediatric unit.

I did not see the Queen until she arrived in Calgary after the Red Deer visit. The main purpose of her Calgary visit was to make presentations to her two militia units, the Calgary Highlanders and the King's Own, both armoured corps regiments. However, I did see her when, at the invitation of the Calgary Military Museum Society, she visited and opened the Museum of the Regiments at Currie Barracks.

The visit began with a luncheon in the Princess Patricia's Canadian Light Infantry Officers' Mess with members of the museum society and officers of the regiments and their spouses. Colleen attended with me. She had missed the reception aboard the *Britannia* in Wolf's Cove.

Following the luncheon, the Queen officially opened the museum and then did a "walk about" in the museum's park. She stopped to speak to me, commenting on the museum and the turnout of guests. Our two conversations had come 31 years apart and she was just as charming as ever.

Planning a visit begins many months before the event. A federal government committee, working with Buckingham Palace representatives, plan for security, transportation, accommodation, the Royal Couple's timed-to-the-minute schedule, the events to take place at each visited place, who will accompany them, who will meet and greet them, and texts for speeches the Queen will deliver. It involves a seemingly endless list of details.

PR planning includes accreditation of the media representatives and provision of official identification for each person that must be produced on request. It also means selecting the best photo locations for both cameramen and photographers and arranging communications for the reporters to enable them to transmit their stories to their respective newspapers and broadcasting stations. It means selecting and preparing individuals to brief the reporters before events. Generally there is at least one briefing each active day of the visit.

The planning works down to each municipality months before the event. It is demanding work. I've always marvelled at the precision and outward calm with each visit.

PART TWO

THE PUBLIC SECTOR

CHAPTER 9

INFORMATION CANADA

Fragmentation of the term "public relations" with such substitutes as "public affairs" is only a change in terms. The function has existed for centuries, but it wasn't called public relations.

From the founding of New France until late in the 19th century, Canadian PR was designed and directed at citizens outside our country – potential settlers living abroad. For nearly 200 years Canadian public relations sought to obtain immigrants to develop the land and build a nation.

Samuel de Champlain made extensive use of France's journals while trying to establish Port Royal in 1604 and when he founded Quebec City in 1608. The Scottish segment of Canada's population owes much to the novelist John Galt, who founded the Canada Company to recruit and aid immigrants, and to Lord Selkirk, a publisher and writer who brought settlers to what is now Manitoba. Their first kirk still stands on the shore of the Red River. Canada's founding father, Sir John A. Macdonald, participated in a public relations campaign even before he became a parliamentarian. As secretary of Kingston's Celtic Society, he advertised an essay contest on "Why Canada Is A Good Place to Live." The winning essay was to be used to publicize Canada in the Old Country.

About 1880 the records of what is now the federal Department of Immigration and Employment indicate that a John Donaldson probably was the first government publicist. He reported his activities in Ireland and Scotland to the minister of emigration. (Perhaps it was he who enticed my ancestors to come to Canada during the potato famines in Ireland.)

That same year, 1880, a former journalist reported to the Canadian Government offices in London to publicize Canada and attract immigrants, using modern methods. He had five travelling exhibits – two of which were motorized! They displayed such Canadian products as stocks of wheat, oats, barley, and apples. On arrival in a community, posters were put on display announcing the place and time a lecture on Canada would be given and that the lecture would be illustrated by the use of a "magic lantern!" Following each lecture, pamphlets about Canada were distributed.

Groups of United Kingdom farmers and clergymen participated in sponsored visits to Canada. Copies of the clergy's comments were sent to virtually every clergyman in the United Kingdom, and more than a million copies of the visiting farmers' comments were sent to citizens in England, Ireland, Scotland, and Wales.

These campaigns were not only launched in Europe. In 1903 more than 30,000 Americans were granted free homesteads of 160 acres. Some of the promotional advertising stretched the truth. One ad read: "Free homestead lands of Western Canada! Magnificent climate! Farmers ploughing in their shirtsleeves in the middle of November." The ad was for Prairie homesteads!

In 1886 the government began to turn its attention to informing the people at home. The Experimental Farm Station Act of 1886 provided for the creation of experimental farms "for the promotion of agriculture by the dissemination of useful and practical information."

In 1907 what is now the Department of Energy, Mines and Resources (EMR) established an information section to issue reports on scientific research. Early in 1973 EMR's scientific research publishing program had a budget of about three-quarters of a million dollars. Today its magazine, *GEOS*, devoted to the earth sciences, is closely followed by the nations of the world.

A publicity and statistics division was established by the Department of National Health in 1920. This division kept doctors informed about scientific research and also provided useful health information to the public. The statistics were a form of research that enabled the department to identify epidemics, their location, and cause.

These PR activities were non-political. Before and for some years after Confederation, the political parties in some instances owned or heavily financed the means of communication – the newspapers of the day. Sir John A.'s great opponent, George Brown, owned the *Toronto Globe*, and it wouldn't be difficult to conclude which party one of Canada's oldest

English-language newspapers, The *Kingston Whig Standard*, supported. Thus, political factors were handled by the newspapers and the politicians themselves who had direct uncomplicated communication, virtually eyeball-to-eyeball, with the electorate. My father's two maiden aunts, residents of Kingston, received personal visits from Macdonald as he kept in touch with his constituents. The National Press Gallery, numbering about twelve year-round members, had much more contact with cabinet ministers.

With the outbreak of the Second World War, nearly every federal government department was carrying out public relations functions and providing information not only directly to the public, but also to newspapers and radio stations. But the war changed the nature of Canada and PR. What had been an agricultural nation became, almost unnoticed by its citizens and governments, one of the world's leading industrial nations. The scope of public relations in the public and private sectors expanded rapidly, and during the war government PR underwent a degree of centralization. This is important to remember now and for the future. Canadian government public relations came of age in the Second World War as did PR in the private sector.

The Bureau of Public Information was created. Posters, articles, photos, and film were directed to the USA (not at war), to Canadians, and to our Allies, telling of Canada's war effort. Canadians on a per capita basis outproduced the United States in the production of arms and munitions. Two hundred speakers addressed U.S. Kiwanis clubs. These speakers told club members why Canada was at war and the extent of Canada's war effort.

By 1944 the federal government was employing 396 "publicity officers," of whom 156 were with the Wartime Information Board. Charles Vinning, friend of Mackenzie King, completed a study for the prime minister which recommended that external and domestic war effort information be combined in a single agency. The amalgamation took place in 1942 when the Wartime Information Board absorbed the Bureau of Public Information. The board also acquired control over printing and distribution of all government publications.

This centralization backfired! It drew strong criticism. Prime Minister King declared the board was not encroaching on department services but "had the duty of seeing to it that in consultation with the departmental officers concerned, wastage of effort is kept within limits, campaigns related, and contradictions avoided." John Grierson, Vinning's successor at the board, in responding to critics in April 1943, said the board's objective was "to develop an overall contact with the public without which Ottawa cannot expect to keep adequately in touch with the people." The board insisted that it was not created to supplant departmental services (shades of Information Canada in the future) but to assist them in coordinating their information programs.

In September 1945 after the war ended, the board was transformed into the Canadian Information Service and transferred to the External Affairs department where it disappeared into oblivion. The federal government recognized the pressures of war that stimulated unity of purpose. Objectives were no longer a factor and the cut and thrust of partisan politics had returned to Parliament. A highly centralized office of information could easily become a serious embarrassment to the party in power. Meanwhile, individual departmental PR services were expanding and new ones created where none previously existed.

After the war most public relations officers, civilian and military, returned to their pre-war employers and stimulated the function there.

In the public sector, expansion almost ran rampant. But there was no overall policy and procedure guidelines and virtually no training in the federal departments. In 1962, the Glassco Commission on Government Organization carried out the first detailed examination of public relations within the federal government. The commission's report was quick to recognize the importance and visibility of the public relations role. "In its broadest sense," the report said, "the provision of information to the public is an integral part of the day-to-day working relation between all levels of the federal government and the Canadian public."

Government operations were becoming more complex. This increased the need not only for the public, but also unions, business, and industry to know government policies and programs. In addition, they were demanding more information. Government was involving itself more and more in the economy and in people's lives. The government had witnessed the increased use of PR techniques by business and industry and followed suit. PR activities by firms praised their products, policies, and programs. The commission stressed that this was not appropriate for government departments. "An important distinction," the report said, "should be drawn between material to which genuinely informs and that which is calculated only to impress; the latter has no place in the information of government."

Today most government PR departments are referred to as Information Services. Thus, the report accelerated the trend away from the term public relations. Although opposed to some PR techniques, the commission did not rule out the necessity, in many instances, for departments to persuade the public. Health and Welfare, Fisheries, Agriculture and Energy, Mines and Resources are examples.

"In certain situations," the commission said, "operations of government can be assisted and their value enhanced when public cooperation is enlisted. In these cases, a properly directed information program proves to be an invaluable aid to the economy and efficiency of government." It cited the value of advertising campaigns to stimulate early income tax returns. However, the commission expressed the view that "when departments take the initiative in publicizing their operations, the proper limits of their information activity becomes debatable." It added: "Aggressive efforts to capture public attention constitute, regardless of intent, attempts to win public support. When this occurs, government information services become active participants in the political process."

The report singled out the armed services as having the largest information service, comprised of 67 officers, 67 other ranks, and 56 civilians. It was also critical of the volume of news releases and the use of the term "public relations."

While the commission recognized some advantages in centralizing information, it came down more on the side of decentralization. It felt that an element of rivalry between departments was "natural and proper," and it suggested that fragmentation of the information function could be reassuring. The point was well made but not appreciated by the authors of the Task Force on Government Information, which produced its report in 1969, seven years after the Glassco Report.

The contrast between the 1962 and 1969 reports was remarkable, as was the response of the federal public relations community. Departmental Information Services generated little adverse criticism of the Glassco Report, whose recommendations they were slow to adopt. The Task Force on Government Information was a different matter!

The Information Service Management Institute of the Federal Institute of Management formed a committee in 1969 to do six studies and meld them into one to be presented to the Task Force. I was assigned the task of condensing the study papers and writing the brief, with assistance from W.S. Drinkwater, J.L. de Lorimier, and James Anderson. A steering committee of D.R. Monk, B.M. Erb, and Louis Racine did the final review of the brief before it was presented to D'Iberville Fortier, chairman of the Task Force.

The brief was entitled "A Look from the Inside." It called for the creation of an information policy; selection standards; training; directors of information to report to the deputy minister or equivalent; membership for directors of information on departmental management committees; and for coordination of federal-provincial information programs by the Privy Council office.

The final Task Force report referred to the more than "50 well informed recommendations contained in 'A Look From The Inside.' The Task Force report, entitled *To Know and Be Known* and published in two volumes, raised a storm. Although it incorporated in one form or another many of the recommendations made by the information officers themselves, it described the Information Services in these words: They had "tolerated bungling, nurtured professional lassitude, lent security to incompetence and allowed supreme disorder."

The strategy was simple. It was thought that highly colourful and volatile text was needed to capture media and public attention. Once the public was convinced, implementation of the report would follow.

It worked, but at a high cost. Information officers, their superior officers, deputy ministers, assistant deputy ministers and directors, and even Members of Parliament of all parties had been alienated. The MPs were suspicious of Info Canada's true role. Would it get between them and their constituents?

The media's reaction was mixed but weighted towards opposition to the proposed agency. Columnist Anthony Westall took an even-handed approach. He reported Information Canada wanted to shake off the idea that it was a propaganda agency for the federal government. But, he wrote, "just what it is going to become is still misty ... they see their task, in part, as continuing what the Commission started, encouraging a sense of Canadian unity to counter the regionalism which pulls the country apart."

Maurice Western of F.P. Publications was a hard-hitting critic of the report and Information Canada. "Volume 1," wrote Western, "at first glance appears to be a spoof or zany burlesque. On closer inspection it is evidently an attempt to provide a momentary diversion for street hippies who might, in the normal course of events, be more attracted to sex novels and marijuana." The article ended: "Behind the Task Force, masquerading in the cloak of participatory democracy, is Big Brother, never so active on Parliament Hill."

In April 1970 Information Canada began recruiting staff. Among the recruits were a sprinkling of former members of the Company of Young Canadians – who had proved an embarrassment to the government and were disbanded. Friction between Information Canada and the information officers increased. Information Canada expanded the information officers' group category by obtaining approval to incorporate Enquiry Centre officers into the group. The ISOs saw this measure as a lowering of selection standards which they insisted must be raised.

By August 1972 there were clear signs that Info Canada was in serious trouble. Tom Ford, one of the three members of the Task Force and an author of the report (I believe he had been a journalist in Toronto), told Canadian Press: "The old approach was that Ottawa was misunderstood by the people of Canada, so we had better go out and tell them how great we are – basically that was the notion." It goes directly contrary to the Glassco Commission report and lends considerable credence to Robert Stanfield's charge that Information Canada was in reality a propaganda agency for the Government. Ford recalled the mod posters and pamphlets

(October 30, 1970)

"Sheer genius! Bar and Leaf! . . . like Hammer and Sickle! Crown and Anchor! Ham and Eggs! His and Hers! Laurel and Hardy!"

Len Norris's cartoon on Information Canada, published in the *Vancouver Sun*, 30 October 1970.

Courtesy Len Norris, *Vancouver Sun*.

that marked Information Canada's debut. "We've made mistakes," Ford admitted, "and some of the stuff we've done in the past was a little dumb!" Opponents of Information Canada – and there were a great number – agreed entirely with Ford's admission.

Three years later, in December 1975, Information Canada was told to end its existence by 31 March 1976. It had had five turbulent years. A Treasury Board statement issued at the time of the funeral estimated the saving at $6 million. Information Canada had amassed a staff of 677!

The demise of Information Canada can be attributed to these causes: an inability to convince others that they did not have the objective of taking over and centralizing control of all federal government information; the traditional suspicion and uneasiness felt by journalists towards centralization of government information; the concerns of the Opposition in Parliament that the agency was being used for political purposes; and, finally, attempting to "tell the story" of the federal government, an aspect of government information condemned by the Glassco Commission seven years earlier.

But some good did come of the reports of the Glassco Commission and the Task Force on Government Information. In April 1970, the Cabinet Committee on Culture and Information asked that a career plan and manpower guidelines be produced for the Information Services officers' group. The ISOs formed six teams and produced studies on: Definitions Classification, Organization, Education, Training and Development, and Staffing. The national executive of the Canadian Public Relations Society was briefed on the project because of the mutual interest of the public and private sectors in the training and development of professional information officers and of the possibility of interchanges between these two sectors. The national executive opened doors in the private sector, making it possible to obtain data and statistics for the project.

I was seconded to the Treasury Board to develop and coordinate production of the Career Plan and Manpower Guidelines. A central group of four – J.B.M. Gibson, a classification specialist, and H. Skeleton, both of the Treasury Board, Carol Paumann, a personnel selection specialist of the Public Service Commission, and myself as chairman – selected a study team of information officers from large, medium, and small departments. The teams totalled 60 officers.

Our central group provided guidance for the teams and a list of questions they were asked to answer. We monitored the teams' discussions, held outside working hours.

The teams developed the "Y" theory of PR careers, whereby juniors entered the profession at the bottom of the letter, progressed up the stem to the crotch, where a decision had to be made to progress up the management or specialist routes. The basis of the theory was the reality that not all information officers wanted to become managers. Some wanted to be the best creators of visuals; others, experts in media relations and special events.

Periodically we wrote to all information officers, telling them what it was all about, the progress being made, as well as asking their views. More than 80 letters and many telephone calls were received suggesting ideas that were fed into the study input. The teams met in conference to present and defend each study. The discussion was recorded and from this the central group produced the brief presented to Cabinet. It was approved.

Provincial requests for briefings on the project were provided and I also responded to requests from the British and American civil service and the Public Relations Society of America (PRSA). I travelled to London, England, Washington, D.C., and New York City to explain the plan and guidelines.

Following Cabinet approval of the Career Plan and Manpower Guidelines, training information officers in management and other administrative skills began. Until then, the ISOs were not selected for management training and, when some of them became PR directors, they encountered difficulties. Their information service was represented by an assistant deputy minister, or other line officer, at the department's management committee. After the plan and guidelines were acted upon, ISOs were accepted for management and administration courses.

CHAPTER 10

FAREWELL TO ARMS – NOW, THE PUBLIC SERVICE

When Bill Milroy left the Directorate of Public Relations (Army), he arranged a posting for me to the Emergency Measures Organization (EMO) of the Privy Council office. I joined EMO in December 1960 and was promoted to lieutenant-colonel.

My task was to produce an emergency information plan for peacetime and wartime emergencies. I reported to Brynes Curry, director of EMO. The experience I acquired in wartime and during the Manitoba flood of 1950 proved invaluable.

A major information vehicle was the bi-monthly EMO *National Digest*. A.B. Bruce Stirling joined EMO as my assistant and I appointed him editor. Published in English and French, it provided information on civil emergency planning. It could be obtained by writing EMO in Ottawa. Its readership was primarily individuals engaged in emergency planning at the three levels of government, as well as scientists and technicians interested in the problems that might arise in the event of a nuclear war.

A sampling of articles published includes: "Do We Want Fallout Shelters?", "The Water Engineer and Radioactive Fallout," "The Organization for Disaster in British Columbia," "The City of Calgary Plan for Natural Disaster," "Public Information Lessons of Carla and Redramp," and "Emergency Health Planning." The Digest also published articles on emergency planning in other countries, such as Great Britain, the United States, and France.

When the author left the Department of Manpower and Immigration (now Manpower and Employment), staff of the Public Relations Branch presented him with a book entitled JDD A *Light Look*. It contained cartoons of projects he had been engaged in before joining Manpower and Immigration. Ken Whitefield produced these cartoons.

In planning for wartime information, I sought the advice of Gillis Purcell, head of Canadian Press, and R.S. (Dick) Malone, publisher of the *Winnipeg Free Press* and my commanding officer in northwest Europe during the war. From them and the EMO staff officers, I developed the plan for Emergency Public Information Services (EPIS). Like the information on fallout shelters, it has never been used. I do not regret the efforts made in producing pamphlets on shelters and how they should be stocked. I believe they would have helped some to survive. Others may contest that view, but I'm satisfied it didn't have to be tested.

What I do know is that the work of EMO staff made major contributions to the establishment of effective peacetime emergency services. Today municipalities across Canada periodically hold simulated exercises to test their emergency services. Canadians are better prepared to meet emergencies now than they were in 1960.

The work at EMO was interesting. I had the support of Brynes Curry and his staff and the satisfaction of having the legendary clerk of the Privy Council, R.B. Bryce, tell me he was pleased with the peacetime and wartime plans.

On instructions from Curry, I sent a draft copy of EPIS to Bryce. A few days later, his secretary called to say he would see me the next day. When I reported to him, his secretary ushered me into the office of the man who held the appointment considered to be the most senior in the federal public service. I was both impressed and nervous. I was even more impressed when he told his secretary to hold all calls, except those from the prime minister.

As I sat down, I saw the copy of EPIS laying on his desk. He leaned over and asked me to tell him about EPIS. I talked for nearly 10 minutes, describing the highlights of the plan. He watched me closely the entire time. When I fell silent, there was a pause of several seconds (it seemed longer) while he looked at me and said nothing. Then he said, "You have solved a problem about which I have been concerned for some time."

With that approval, EPIS was officially adopted.

He accompanied me to the office door and said goodbye. I floated all the way back to EMO's offices.

I was, however, happy to return to the army as director of public relations, an appointment for which I felt prepared. But my happiness was to be short-lived.

Late in November 1964, when unification of the armed services was instituted, I requested retirement because, although I agreed with integration, I disagreed with unification. Unification authorities granted my request and I received my release 48 hours later.

An irritant was my official goodbye letter, thanking me for my 23 years of service: it was signed by an Air Force officer. However, this was eased somewhat by a personal letter from Adjutant General Bill Anderson.

When I was leaving the army I had a call from Brynes Curry and, at his request, I visited his office. He was now assistant deputy minister of the newly organized Department of Manpower and Immigration (now Employment and Immigration). He asked that I join the department and fashion an information service. I agreed, stating I would spend 12 months on the task and then enter the private sector.

A new minister was appointed and he brought the director of Information Services of the post office with him, B.M. Erb, whom I welcomed to the department. Erb started me down the road to becoming a civilian once more.

An early project was to implement the information plan for a White Paper on immigration. Criticism of the selection standards for immigrants and the decisions of immigration officers in Canadian embassies abroad resulted in the government directing the department to review its standards and propose improvements.

The White Paper provided broad new principles for selection which were debated and discussed in Parliament and by the public, especially those community organizations having a special interest in the subject.

The launching of the White Paper provided me with an opportunity to see the government information function operating when new legislation was being proposed. Initially an Information Services paper on the origin of the White Paper and the reasons for its presentation was distributed to immigration offices in Canada and abroad to enable the staff to answer local news media queries prior to release of the White Paper upon presentation in the House of Commons.

Members of the Parliamentary Press Gallery obtained copies in the "locked room" two hours before the document was presented in the House. Departmental officials were available to answer questions. The minister joined them about 30 minutes before going to the House. He made a statement about the White Paper and then answered questions.

When he rose in the House to present the paper, the reporters were free to leave the locked room. Simultaneously, telex summaries, containing White Paper highlights and information important to specific countries, were sent to the heads of Canadian missions and immigration officers abroad.

Information to the Canadian public was concerned with informing ethnic groups wishing to sponsor relatives, updating employers seeking staff from abroad, and assisting newly arrived immigrants by directing pertinent information to the ethnic press.

Discussion of the White Paper lasted about nine months. From these discussions, new immigration regulations were formulated and tabled in the House of Commons. The information program was more complex. Its purpose was to support management in the introduction of the regulations. The primary objective was to gain understanding and earn the support of the interested publics in the new regulations and their application. Special publics included business and industry, ethnic groups wishing to bring relatives to Canada, and provincial governments.

However, the new regulations still were being formulated and the information plan for their announcement was completed 8 August 1967. I was appointed as project officer for the information function.

Members of the Information Services were assigned managers who were developing the regulations. Integration of the Information Services officers (ISO) with the planners resulted in the production of an information kit for the media and Canadian immigration officers overseas. All items were approved by management before the kits were assembled. They contained:

a)   Regulations on landing requirements for immigrants.
b)   The minister's statement to the Parliamentary Committee.
c)   A news release describing the new selection regulations.
d)   Background notes.
e)   A leaflet on the regulations, containing sufficient information to meet initial inquiries for those interested in sponsoring relatives, and non-immigrants interested in applying for landed immigrant status.
f)   Guidance for handling media inquiries.

The press kit contained only items (a) to (d), inclusive. Item (f) was for the use of information officers in Canada and abroad who were likely to receive inquiries from the media. The kit was also provided to social and welfare agencies, Canadian transportation companies, foreign travel agencies, foreign transportation companies, and, through the Department of External Affairs, diplomatic representatives of foreign governments.

Advertising in the Canadian media drew the attention of the

Canadian public to the availability of the leaflet. Detailed advertising of the new regulations would have been costly and, because of the technical language, likely would fail to gain readership perception.

The minister held a news conference in the National Press Centre to describe the new regulations and answer questions.

Reaction to the new regulations was favourable. While the information plan had proved effective, acceptance of the regulations can be attributed to the fact that they were less rigid. Before the change was made, selection of immigrants was based on occupational skills and level of education. These two factors were retained, but added were personal qualities, occupational demand, age, employment arrangements, knowledge of English and/or French, presence of relatives in Canada, and area of destination.

The department also carried out an information program abroad, with the objective of influencing high-calibre immigrants to select Canada as their country of destination. Overseas regional directors were responsible for advertising in Britain, France, and other European countries. I provided counselling and guidance.

After touring Europe, I initiated the production of a series of pamphlets on life in Canada. They were produced in French, English, and a variety of foreign languages. They were not a success. Officers counselling immigrants felt the pamphlets presented too rosy a picture of life in Canada. These same officers, nonetheless, were highly effective in informing prospective immigrants, and the department had many letters from individuals who had immigrated to Canada and had been helped by their wise counsel. For me, it was a lesson learned.

Fundamentally, the overseas program mirrored the first information efforts in the late-1800s and early-1900s. Exhibits were mounted at fairs and audio-visual productions were provided by Information Services for use abroad. The department also sponsored visits to Canada of selected media representatives.

From Manpower and Immigration, I was transferred to the Department of Energy, Mines and Resources (EMR) in April 1969. Erb had left to join Information Canada, and a new deputy minister of manpower and immigration insisted on having a bilingual director of Information Services. The EMR director was bilingual and we played musical chairs — for him a lateral transfer and for me a promotion because I had been assistant director to Erb.

While Manpower and Immigration had been interesting, it found me facing the problem of being converted to civilian life and adjusting to operating in the bureaucracy. At times, it wasn't easy. I discovered I couldn't have the last word on the posting of information officers. In Ottawa I had an officer of long service who had served me well. I had hoped to use the foreign service postings of London and Geneva as positions for the information officers to expand their experience.

The incumbent in London had been enjoying the posting when I felt it was time for him to return to Canada to be replaced with an officer who I considered had served well and needed the experience abroad to equip him for further advancement in his career. The regional director in London wanted to retain the information officer he had. His wishes prevailed. I was able, however, to recruit and post an information officer to Geneva, the department's European headquarters.

I was with EMR only about two months when work began on the Canada Water Act, which was to be tabled on 25 August 1969.

The distribution of information concerning new legislation is a frequent task of government departments. The rights of Parliament must be respected and details of the proposed legislation must first be made public in the House of Commons. At the same time, it is important to inform not only the general public, but groups having a special interest (i.e., other governments, environmentalists, and leaders of the opposition). This helps to avoid the distortion that can result from public and political verbal conflict. The Canada Water Act provided an opportunity to experiment with distribution of such information.

Under the British North America Act, land was given to the provinces; they later acquired the water within their boundaries. The power over water was shared with the federal government, which was responsible for navigation, fisheries, and agricultural usage. This responsibility covered lakes and rivers which straddled interprovincial and international boundaries. With the increase in environmental problems, water pollution was seen as a matter of national urgency, and the public were becoming impatient.

In 1966, under the Government Reorganization Act, EMR was given a mandate to establish a national water policy and program in close cooperation with the provinces. The many public announcements and statements made by government officials (federal and provincial), the continuing press coverage and editorial comment on matters related to water conservation and improvement, public discussion and, at times, outcry on the subject, created an atmosphere of expectancy and intense public interest.

I anticipated reportage would occur spontaneously in the days immediately prior to introduction of the act. This happened, and the department's information officers and I responded to media queries, bearing in mind that specific details of the act could not be released.

The objectives of the information plan were to provide effective dissemination about the act and its significance to the development, improvement, and management of Canada's water resources. By cooperating fully with the media and providing complete information about the act, we endeavoured to encourage accuracy and in-depth reporting. Finally, we hoped to encourage public discussion and understanding of the act through the stories and editorials produced by the media.

The information to be distributed – copies of the act, a news release, the minister's statement to be made in the House and its highlights – was packaged in a news kit.

Responsibility for producing the information-kit documents was assigned to individual information officers as follows:

John MacLeod, my assistant director, and myself, in consultation with the assistant deputy minister (Water), prepared a background paper interpreting and explaining the act. MacLeod and I also prepared a fact sheet itemizing highlights and key clauses for reporters, information officers, and other departments. I also involved myself in the preparation of television clips and radio tapes of the minister to be tied into newscasts.

ISO Phil Cooper prepared historical information on water policies and programs in Canada leading to the development of the Canada Water Act.

ISO George Classen wrote a résumé of constitutional implications of the act and its effect on governments at all levels – federal, provincial, and municipal.

ISO Tony Goodson, the Information Services artist, produced a diagram showing the make-up of the proposed Canada Water Advisory Board and a folder for each kit's documents.

The minister at this time was Otto E. Lang, who was substituting for the seriously ill J.J. Greene.

In an effort to reduce distortion to a minimum and because of Canada's vast distances, copies of the kit were pre-positioned in major populace centres and, on signal from the department, delivered by security agencies simultaneously across Canada. This was the distribution list:

Parliament
1. Cabinet
2. Leaders of Opposition
3. House of Commons
4. Senate

Government	1.	Deputy heads of federal departments
	2.	Information directors, National Health and Welfare, Fisheries, Fisheries Research Board
	3.	Provincial resource ministers
	4.	Selected municipal organizations
Associations	1.	Conservation organizations
	2.	Youth groups
	3.	Outdoor associations
	4.	Religious organizations (Canadian headquarters)

Universities and Research Organizations

News Media	1.	Press gallery
	2.	Dailies, French and English
	3.	Weeklies, French and English
	4.	Radio stations, French and English
	5.	Television stations, French and English
	6.	Religious press: selected consumer, trade, and technical magazines
Departmental	1.	Minister's office
	2.	Deputy minister's office
	3.	ADM's and senior officers
	4.	Directors
	5.	Canadian Centre Inland Waters
	6.	Regional offices in Calgary, Vancouver, and Victoria

The deliveries coincided with the commencement of the Ottawa news conference which began immediately after Minister Otto Lang completed his statement in the House. All totalled, there were 2,400 English and 700 French kits. Subsequently, 1,500 English and 400 French kits were distributed.

More than 50 correspondents attended the news conference. Each was given the kit on the proposed legislation. The correspondents arrived 25 minutes before Mr. Lang. This provided them with an opportunity to read the contents of the kit and ask technical questions of a department panel of experts, thus better preparing them for the session with Lang.

In addition to the prepositioning of the kits and the Ottawa news conference – which resulted in print and broadcast coverage out of the national capital – special arrangements were made for a whirlwind ministerial coast-to-coast trip.

Lang, along with departmental officials and myself, flew by Department of Transport aircraft to each provincial capital in successive days. On arrival, the minister would first meet with provincial officials, after which a news conference or visits to the media would begin. Some provincial authorities would participate.

In Quebec the meeting was not held in the legislative building, but in a motel in Ste. Foy on the outskirts of the city. There were no reporters present nor was the minister interviewed by the media.

The Quebec meeting followed a morning meeting in the Ontario legislative buildings the morning after the tabling in the House. The Ste. Foy meeting followed in the afternoon. We then flew to Newfoundland where I saw Premier Joey Smallwood for the second time.

I had accompanied Brigadier Walsh when he toured the reserve companies of the 27th Brigade in the fall of 1951. He paid a courtesy call on Premier Smallwood, to whom I was introduced. I sat in the outer office chatting with the commissioner during the visit.

The commissioner referred to Canada and Canadians as if Newfoundland's "Father of Confederation" hadn't fulfilled what he likely considered the greatest accomplishment of his political career. At the airport a sign read: "Flights to Canada."

With Lang, I attended the meeting with Premier Smallwood and some of the provincial cabinet ministers and officials. From the meeting we went with the premier to a news conference.

From Newfoundland we went on to the Maritime provincial capitals and then touched base in all of the western provinces, with a round of meetings and media conferences at each. The results were quite remarkable, primarily because of media interest in the subject. The full support the department and the minister gave to the media contributed to the quality and quantity of the reportage.

In addition to a television news clip prepared by the Information Service and sent to 35 stations and used by 30, Lang appeared live on CBC-TV and radio networks five consecutive evenings, and on CTV National News four consecutive nights. The story also was accorded nine of the 29 minutes of the CBC radio program, "The World at Six."

Gordon Sinclair, of "Front Page Challenge," dismissed the subject on CFRB with one sentence, to the effect that it was much ado about nothing.

But nearly every French and English daily newspaper published the story on page one, top fold. The majority of editorials praised the proposed legislation. There also was some healthy criticism. The Vancouver *Province* editorialized, "The mere setting of standards is not enough to keep pollution from becoming an increasing problem. There is one lesson to be gained from the history of pollution control, it is this: something better must be found and so far – the new federal proposals included – we don't seem to have found it."

In my final report to the deputy minister, I commented that "the information plan contributed to the clarity of the discussions and reporting of the proposed legislation. The technique can be duplicated for proposed government policy of major importance to the general public."

CHAPTER 11

HUDSON 70

In 1970, my second year with Energy, Mines and Resources, ships occupied much of the Information Services' time. EMR had a Marine Sciences Branch and the Bedford Institute of Oceanography in Dartmouth, Nova Scotia. The institute operates Canada's fleet of scientific ships, the flagship of which is the Canadian Scientific Ship (CSS) *Hudson*.

CSS *Hudson* left Halifax 19 November 1969, on a major one-year oceanographic expedition called Hudson 70. The *Hudson*, the only ship outside of Russia that was designed and built to facilitate scientific studies, was the first ship to circumnavigate North and South America. The 122 scientists on the voyage were mainly from Canadian government laboratories. American, Argentinian, and Chilean scientists joined the expedition at various points of call. The scientists carried out studies of the waters of four oceans: Atlantic, Antarctic, Pacific, and Arctic.

The objective of the expedition was to obtain knowledge of the oceans valuable to the development of the underseas resources of Canada and the world. Canadian oceanographic studies were accelerated in the 1960s for economic and military reasons.

About five months before Hudson left Halifax, an American Arctic expedition was launched. The giant oil tanker USS *Manhattan* sailed into Canadian Arctic waters "to collect scientific data necessary to assess the economic and operational feasibility of a year-round arctic marine operation."

In Prudhoe Bay exploratory drilling had discovered a vast oil reserve. Pipelines are difficult to install in the Arctic where the frozen tundra occasionally thaws. Tankers could haul the oil from Prudhoe Bay through the Northwest Passage, if such a trip was feasible. If the experiment succeeded,

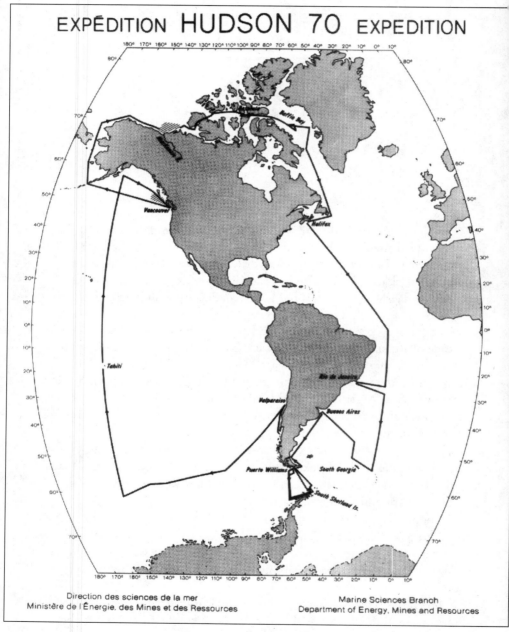

Courtesy Department of Energy, Mines and Resources.

it would open up exploitation of Canada's vast Arctic resources. And North America and European markets would have a decided economic edge on pipeline transportation if the *Manhattan* succeeded.

While the government designated the Department of Transportation as having primary interest in the *Manhattan*'s voyage, I was assigned to chair a committee of the other interested departments: External Affairs, Indian Affairs and Northern Development, EMR, as well as Transport. The main task was to coordinate the production of an information kit incorporating each department's historical background and responsibilities in the Arctic.

The purpose was to have information available if the Canadian or American media expressed interest. International convention demands that for a nation to claim rights over the continental shelf, they must demonstrate a preparedness to explore and develop the shelf. Our continental shelf is almost as big as our country. The kits produced contained ample evidence that Canada had explored and was developing the shelf.

Plotting the *Hudson*'s course. Left to right, geologist-biologist Gus Vilks, whose studies proved that Arctic waters flow in from the Atlantic and that the Canadian North is consequently affected by any pollution in the North Atlantic; Captain Dave Butler, skipper of the *Hudson*; geologist Dr. Bernard Pelletier, whose research changed the face of northern development by disclosing the terrible risk of employing oil tankers in Arctic waters; and Roy Gould, navigating officer.
Courtesy Marine Sciences Branch, Department of Energy, Mines and Resources.

The cover of the kit displayed the Canadian flag and below it the title in both languages "Canada in the North • le Canada et le Grand nord."

I did not become involved with the PR aspects of *Manhattan*, but the voyage of the *Hudson* resulted in startling scientific evidence that affected the objective of the American ship.

Planning for the scientific aspects of Hudson 70 had been underway for three years. The PR planning for the expedition began about the same time the *Manhattan* sailed. The information kit was produced by John MacLeod and Douglas Shenstone, senior editor of the Information Services, with the aid of departmental scientists. Shenstone headed up a small staff of editors that not only prepared news releases but edited scientific papers. Their skills contributed to the clarity of the kit's documents.

Following is an excerpt from a three-page release that illustrates the clarity of the writing, enabling non-scientific minds to comprehend the work of the scientists:

In the South Atlantic, South Pacific and Antarctic Oceans, studies of biological and chemical features of the oceans

Shipboard science has little in common with clinically clean laboratory research. Samples of sedimentary mud are dredged from the seabed and dumped on the deck for the scientist to analyze.

Courtesy Marine Sciences Branch, Department of Energy, Mines and Resources.

and the way they are influenced by the movements of large masses of water and ocean currents form the main part of the program. Massive sinking of water in the Weddell Sea provides cold water which fills the deeps of the oceans as far north in the Atlantic as the Grand Banks of Newfoundland. A secondary sinking of water at latitudes of 50° south around the Antarctic Continent provides a layer at intermediate depths which extends into the North Atlantic. Since only the most general features of this primary circulation of the deep Atlantic are known, these water movements will be studied by the physical oceanographers, and the biological life and nutrients associated with them by the biologists and chemists aboard.

An incident occurred two days before *Hudson* sailed in November that could have delayed the departure by as much as three months. The ship had left the Bedford Institute dock and sailed down the Halifax Harbour to the fuelling dock. A heavy fog developed and, as the ship was returning that night to its home berth, a collision with a fuel barge was avoided with only six inches to spare. I did not learn of the incident until the expedition ended a year later. There's a PR lesson here for non-PR managers: Keep your PR director or his or her branch informed.

The expedition presented a formidable problem for the Information Services. It was brought sharply to my mind when, attending a CPRS luncheon after the ship sailed, I recognized that some individuals felt sufficient information about Hudson 70 was not reaching the public. An out-of-town member, not realizing my position with EMR, suggested a camera crew should have sailed with the ship. I explained that underwater motion picture film suitable for a production was unobtainable because the waters in which the research was taking place was too opaque and film of ocean floor samples doesn't make for good movies.

The minister's office had come to our rescue by arranging with the publishers McClelland and Stewart to have author Alan Edmonds accompany the expedition, which resulted in *Voyage to the Edge of the World*. Still, that wasn't off the press until 1973, and newsworthy items were unlikely to be available until the ship returned to Halifax.

The success of the measurements of the flow and variation of the flow at Cape Horn provided the break we needed. The chief scientist aboard *Hudson*, Dr. Cedric Mann, had, with American scientists, endeavoured to do such measurements between Iceland and Greenland. The experiment failed.

For more than two years, Dr. Mann and technicians at the Bedford Institute worked on perfecting instruments that would bring success. EMR in Ottawa received the word that they had indeed succeeded and that the findings might ultimately affect all living beings on the planet. And what was vitally important to the PR services, the scientists were prepared to say so.

A replacement crew for the *Hudson* had been planned when it reached Valparaiso after having made calls at Rio de Janeiro, Buenos Aires, Punta Arenas, and Puerto Williams. I recommended that Deputy Minister Jack Austin (now a senator) request that EMR's minister, the Hon. J.J. Greene, speak to the minister of defence to provide an aircraft to fly the substitute crew from Halifax to Valparaiso. There would be space for a party of reporters and a few department officials. It worked.

I sent one of the Information Services best writers, Mary Giroux, now a member of the Providence Sisters of Charity of Kingston, on ahead via Mexico City to Santiago, Chile, where she worked with Canadian External Affairs to prepare for the reporters' arrival and movement to the port on the coast.

Invitations were extended to the media. The priority was given to newswire services, broadcasting networks, and newspapers with large circulations. More than a dozen acceptances were received.

The flight with the media representatives took off from Ottawa, landed in Halifax to pick up the substitute crew, flew to Kingston, Jamaica, for an overnight stopover, and then to Santiago for another overnight stay, before moving on to Valparaiso by road.

Mary Giroux met us at the airport and, considering the predicament she'd faced, she had done an excellent job preparing the way for the reporters. After a few days, External Affairs had helped provide the essential clothes and toilette articles she needed. Compounding her problems, her baggage had been off-loaded in error during a stopover in Mexico City.

On arrival in Valparaiso, a news conference was held aboard the *Hudson*. Dr. William Cameron, director of Marine Services, EMR, coined the phrase "taking the pulse of the oceans" to describe the work of Dr. Mann. It was an apt description. Some scientists believe there is a remarkable similarity between our circulatory system and that of the oceans, the pulse being the Antarctic Ocean, which swirls around that continent, mixing the waters of the Pacific, Atlantic, and Indian Oceans.

css *Hudson* in the Arctic.
Courtesy Department of Energy, Mines and Resources.

css *Hudson* returns to the dock of the Marine Sciences Branch of the Department of Energy, Mines and Resources in Dartmouth, Nova Scotia, after circumnavigating South and North America.
Courtesy Marine Sciences Branch, Department of Energy, Mines and Resources.

Bo'sun Joe Avery made this plaque as the *Hudson* headed down to the Antarctic.
Unable to find a place to erect it there, he finally set it up a few miles outside
Resolute in the Canadian Arctic. Aided by geologist Dr. Bernard Pelletier, he
drilled holes in a massive rock, cemented steel posts in place, then riveted the
plaque to the posts.

Courtesy Marine Sciences Branch, Department of Energy, Mines and Resources.

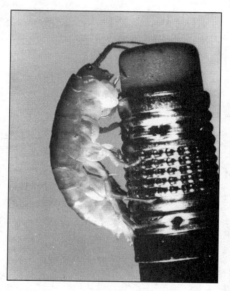

Here, magnified considerably, is the major find of Dr. Ed Bousfield of Ottawa.
"From one beach in the archipelago," an EMR pamphlet reported, "he collected
four species of amphipod, a tiny creature you'd call a beach flea if you met one
sunbathing. One of the four turned out to be at the stage of evolution from
marine creature to land creature that amphipods elsewhere in the world had
reached and passed several million years ago. He called it a living dinosaur."

Courtesy Department Energy, Mines and Resources.

Dr. Mann and some of the other scientists answered questions about the experiment, which had been a triumph of science, instrumentation, and seamanship. A string of meters, specially designed to obtain the readings, had been lowered into the sea at depths as much as three miles. They remained there for several days before being retrieved when the ship returned to where each metre had been sunk.

The reporters had their story and excellent coverage resulted, some of it international.

From Valparaiso, the *Hudson*'s ports of call were Tahiti, Vancouver, and Victoria. The expedition entered the Beaufort Sea 24 August 1970 and spent about a month in the Northwest Passage carrying out more scientific studies before returning to Halifax on 16 October 1970.

Eight days earlier, I had been transferred temporarily with my secretary, Alice Trudel, to the Treasury Board to head up the central planning group to develop and coordinate a career plan and manpower policy guidelines for federal public service information officers. As a result, John MacLeod and Doug Shenstone planned for the news conference on the *Hudson*'s arrival in Halifax on the Hudson's arrival.

The background paper covered physical oceanography, biology, chemistry, Chilean fjords, hydrography, and geophysics. It was lengthy and detailed, describing the scientists' findings in terms a lay person could understand.

Having been involved from the start of the expedition, I was delighted when invited to be present in Halifax for the return of the *Hudson* and the subsequent news conference.

The following are just a few of the highlights:

- The charting of the Beaufort Sea resulted in accurate navigational charts. The work had come about as a consequence of the petroleum discoveries in the area. The work of the scientists resulted in stringent precautions to prevent oil pollution of our offshore waters.
- The biologists found two 300-mile-wide bands of fish in the South Atlantic and South Pacific. Concentrations of fish four to five inches long were of the order of two tonnes of fish per square mile. In the North Pacific, the distribution was nearly the reverse, with a broad band of approximately one tonne per square mile.
- In the Chilean Fjords, the biologists found animals unique to that part of the world, one-third of which were probably new to science. Some of the animals were similar to those of South Africa, Australia, and New Zealand, lending support to the continental drift theory.

However, the highlight of research in the Beaufort Sea was a surprising and unexpected discovery. An extensive shoal area was discovered 65 miles north of Tuktoyuktuk by the *Manhattan*. Scientists aboard *Hudson* discovered additional shoals across the Gulf of Amundsen at the west end of the Northwest Passage. They were sprinkled with pongos, a sharp undulation of permafrost which had been seen on land. Before the *Hudson*'s voyage, it had never been discovered in the sea. They could have split open the bottom of the USS *Manhattan*! In other oceans, a tanker could navigate around pongos. But a tanker frozen tightly in ice would not be able to navigate and could be drawn over the pongos by the ice in which it was imprisoned, splitting its hull and spilling the oil – a disaster for the sensitive Arctic environment.

The news conference ended on an amusing note, courtesy of Captain David Butler. When asked by a correspondent if he had experienced any moments of serious concern, he paused with a "Jack Benny" sense of timing and replied, "Yes, as we passed down the coast of Labrador ...

The Honourable Joe Green, minister of EMR, presents a plaque to Captain Dave Butler, skipper of the CSS *Hudson*, at voyage end in Halifax to commemorate the ship's circumnavigation of South and North America.
Courtesy Department of Energy, Mines and Resources.

we ran out of tea!" He didn't mention the missed collision two days before the departure.

I had learned once more some fundamentals of PR. Had a news release been issued in Ottawa describing the discoveries off the horn of South America, coverage would have been mediocre. By taking the reporters to Valparaiso, they were able to experience the excitement of the scientists, and they had gained the opportunity to question them. A release would have drawn attention from the science publications, but extensive coverage in the popular press would not have been a certainty.

The best coverage a PR practitioner can obtain depends on the news quality of the story, the ability to bring reporters to the story, and providing them with all the assistance and accurate information possible. Hudson 70 had all three.

PART THREE

THE PRIVATE SECTOR

CHAPTER 12

A PARK FOR ALL SEASONS

About 1971, the federal government announced a formula combining age and years of service to permit early retirement without penalty. By this time, I began to think about trying my wings in the private sector. I had advanced as far as I could in the public sector and was eight years from retirement. I wasn't looking forward to that day. I wanted to continue working in PR. Employment in the private sector would make that possible, and it would provide an entirely new experience. I also wanted to discover if I could succeed in the private sector. I had been in public service for 31 years – 23 in the army and eight in the federal civil service. It was time to move on.

In November 1972, while attending a joint convention of the Canadian Public Relations Society (CPRS) and Public Relations Society of America (PRSA) in the Detroit Windsor area, I made contact with my future employer, though neither of us realized it. The convention hotel was in Detroit. The Canadian event was a black tie dinner in Windsor, with the delegates there moving across the border by bus.

Just as we were about to pull away from the hotel, I caught sight of movement out of the corner of my eye. I turned to look out the window. A black youth of about 14 years of age, rage covering his face, flung himself against the side of the bus and hammered it with clenched fists. The incident shook the delegates.

When Colleen and I boarded the bus in Windsor for the return, it quickly filled up to standing room only. A man grasped the metal handle on the corner of our seat and I looked up. I was wearing a gold, beaver felt, Al Capone-style fedora. And there above me, on another head, was the same hat, only in grey. The man it belonged to was of medium height, in his late-30s or early-40s. He smiled and said, "Good evening."

I recalled a female response to such situations and said, "On you it looks great!" He laughed. No introduction was made.

The incident of the youth remained with me and I followed the news accounts of events in Detroit, which went from bad to worse and, finally, led to major riots. The community leadership took hold and, through strenuous community relations work, the problems were reduced.

Awaiting me on my return to Ottawa from the conventions were requests from Alberta, Ontario, the Northwest Territories, the British government, the United States government, and the Public Relations Society of America for a briefing on the career and manpower plan produced for federal information officers.

The deputy minister of EMR, Jack Austin, approved the carrying out of the briefings. In London and Washington, I met with government officials holding PR appointments, as well as other non-PR managers. In New York, the briefing was given to senior executive employees of PRSA and the PR director of a major insurance company.

In Edmonton, I briefed the head of Alberta's Information Services, David Wood, a national president of CPRS who later was to author *The Lougheed Legacy.*

When our work was done David informed me he was soon returning to his former employer in the private sector in Calgary. I told him I might soon be asking him for a job. The next day, as I was leaving Edmonton to visit an EMR branch in Calgary, David told me he had arranged a meeting for me with John Francis, the president of Francis, Williams & Johnson Ltd., a public relations and advertising consultant. I was to go to the FWJ office from the Calgary airport. I arrived before Francis, whom I thought I'd never met, and waited in the reception area.

A few minutes later I heard the elevator door open and there headed towards the office was the hat, it belonged to Francis. It was a friendly interview. In September 1973, I was offered the job of manager of FWJ public relations. I joined the firm on 1 November for a four-year period. It extended into 12 years because I enjoyed the work. A fascinating project introduced me to work in the private sector.

In October 1966, Calgary city planners unveiled the concept of a park for all seasons. Six years later, the Alberta government offered to purchase land for urban park development, and in 1973 set aside $15 million to develop Fish Creek Provincial Park.

In the fall of 1973, the provincial government appointed a Fish Creek Park Advisory Committee of five: Bill Milne, chairman, and members Nancy Peters, Margaret Southern, Harvey Olsen, and Gerald Heald. The mandate given the committee was: to determine the kind of park Calgarians and southern Albertans wish developed in Fish Creek Valley. What kind of park was it to be? Natural versus recreational; which did Albertans want?

The park proposal was also politically sensitive. Would the city of Calgary accept design decisions made by the province?

The committee commissioned FWJ to develop – at the committee's direction – a master public relations plan to achieve their mandate. The strategy chosen included informing the public about the valley's location, size, and ecology; a scientifically designed survey to determine the kind of park Calgarians and southern Albertans desired; use of the survey results to produce a park design concept; presentation of the design concept to the public; and a public hearing to determine reaction.

The master PR plan's objective was the same as the committee's mandate. From the first weekly meeting between the committee and the consultants, the public relations and advertising planning and programming were completely integrated. This integration was a major contribution to the success of the project.

Francis headed up the FWJ team, attending all meetings of the Advisory Committee. I frequently accompanied him. This gave me the opportunity of observing private sector citizens dealing with PR planning. It also enabled me to learn Francis's approach to counselling. Through education and experience, he combined PR knowledge with managerial skills; thus, he spoke a language the committee members understood. He had obtained a degree in business administration, entering PR for a short time before attending Boston University to obtain a master's degree in PR. He began acquiring managerial skills when he founded FWJ in 1957.

Other members of the team from FWJ's advertising, art, special events, and broadcast production departments attended meetings when the agenda indicated their knowledge would make a contribution. As a result, neither the committee members nor the agency staff were confronted with surprises.

To achieve the objective, it was necessary to:

a. Identify the interested community organizations.
b. Inform these organizations about the committee's appointment and mandate.

c.   Inform the general public about the committee's appointment and mandate.

d.   Inform the general and special publics – primarily environmental groups – about the Fish Creek property, its location, size, and character.

e.   Create a means whereby the general and special publics could make known their wishes concerning the proposed park.

The master plan comprised three major programs:

- advertising;
- information by direct mail, and by means of unpaid space and time obtained from newspaper and broadcasting stations; and
- direct public relations by mail and meetings.

The master plan was implemented in three phases. These were:

Phase I   Informing the special and general publics about the committee's appointment, mandate, and the location, size, and character of Fish Creek Park property.

Phase II   Providing the public with a means of making their wishes known and analyzing that response.

Phase III   Presenting a conceptual design of the park based on the public's desires and listening to the views of individuals and organizations concerning that concept.

Francis presented the PR plan to the committee where it was discussed in detail and approved.

Implementation of Phase I began with identification of 192 organizations having an interest in the project. In some cases the title of an organization indicated its probable sensitivity to the project. For example, the Fish Creek Park Association had worked with the Calgary Field Naturalists' Society and was probably the first organization to mount a concerned public campaign for the park. Included in its membership was a broad spectrum of Calgary community organizations and associations.

A news release was distributed announcing formation of the committee, its purpose, and the names of its members. Letters were drafted and sent to the 192 organizations and to private land owners in the Fish Creek area, the city of Calgary Planning Department, and the City Parks Department.

The two categories of letters defined the Advisory Committee's objective and the three phases of the PR plan. The letter to the private land owners also expressed the committee's concern for the owners' rights and promised it would require those rights be to fully respected by all with whom it communicated. The letters were dated 28 February 1974.

A news conference was held at the Burns's Ranch, an historic site in the heart of the property. A news kit including aerial photographs of Fish Creek Valley was issued and reporters met committee members and were briefed by Chairman Bill Milne.

Following the briefing, the reporters, photographers, and cameramen were flown by helicopter over the park area. The *Calgary Herald* coverage was the first, and it published a full page of colour pictures.

Work began that day by CFAC-TV Calgary on a documentary production to be telecast on 16 June, the day before the public hearing.

Meanwhile, work had begun on a scale contour model of the proposed park area. Accompanied by Fish Creek Valley photographic enlargements, the display was placed in the Calgary Public Library for a three-week period prior to the public being asked to express their wishes concerning the park.

In conjunction with the display, committee members gave informal talks at "brown bag" luncheons in the library auditorium, featuring a slide presentation and ending with a question-and-answer session.

The luncheons were publicized by news releases and public service announcements sent to the newspapers and broadcasting stations. While attendance figures were not recorded, the committee members who participated were satisfied with the numbers of citizens attending their presentation.

Committee members, frequently accompanied by representatives of the 192 identified organizations, appeared on radio and television talk shows such as CFAC-TV's "Our Town," CFCN-TV's "This Week," CTV's "Calgary Eye Opener" and "Home Run," CFCN Radio's "Talk of the Town," and on two open-line programs. They also filled eight speaking engagements at various service clubs, a business association, a school, and a church. They used visual materials to illustrate their presentation, always closing with a question-and-answer period.

The Southern Alberta Institute of Technology (SAIT) and Mount Royal College broadcast Fish Creek Valley programs to students on closed-circuit televisions.

When appropriate, copies of news releases and advance notification of broadcasts were mailed to the 192 organizations. It's impossible to guarantee that a news release will be published, and members of the special groups could easily miss hearing an important announcement. We wanted to ensure that the special interest people were kept as fully informed as possible.

The advertising strategy was to use purchased space and time to tell Calgarians and southern Albertans:

a.   about Fish Creek Park;
b.   that the park would be planned according to the needs and wishes of southern Albertans;
c.   that a questionnaire would be distributed through The *Calgary Herald* and The *Albertan* on 30 March. This ad was designed to start citizens thinking about the park. It invited them to view the park model at the library and told them how the park would be planned; and
d.   to consider their goals for the park.

The main concerns were obtaining the support of the environmental groups. The question of whether the city of Calgary would accept a provincial design couldn't be resolved until the design was created.

The public relations program centred almost exclusively on identifying sensitive organizations and individuals, and ensuring that they were kept informed. As a result of a response from the Fish Creek Park Association, a meeting was arranged between the Advisory Committee members and its association. In this way, the association received, firsthand, a complete explanation of the committee's role and objectives. The committee also promised to keep the association, and through it the Calgary Field Naturalists' Society, fully informed on its plans and programs. This was done by direct mail and telephone, and copies of all news releases issued were directed to the association. The association, as a result, moved from a position of scepticism to a stance that remained in complete support of the committee throughout the project.

Phase II centred on the design of the questionnaire; the means of distribution; stimulating the general and special publics to complete and return the questionnaires; and analyzing and tabulating the results for computerization.

As planning for each of these functions was completed by FWJ, Francis presented each to the committee for discussion and approval.

The combined circulation of the two dailies was 165,000. The response was phenomenal! More than 31,700 questionnaires were returned by Calgary citizens and 35 other Alberta communities. Responses came from five other Canadian provinces, the Yukon and Northwest Territories, four states of the U.S., two United Kingdom cities, Holland, Egypt, Bahamas, and Germany. Fifty-nine percent of respondents had attached additional comments ranging from brief notes to letters of five to ten pages. Every return and every letter was read and its contents tabulated by FWJ staff. The tabulations were then presented to the committee.

The questionnaire itself was comprehensive and detailed to provide worthwhile results. Cartooning provided a light and warm touch.

The first question went straight to the point:

How do you think Fish Creek Provincial Park should be planned? (check the appropriate blank)

_____ A.   As a fully developed park with a wide range of recreational facilities.
_____ B.   As a park with some developed recreational areas and some undeveloped natural setting areas.
_____ C.   A totally undeveloped park retaining its natural setting.

Some of the question headings included Summer Facilities, Winter Facilities; Senior Citizens; Development within the Park for Autos and Snowmobiles, Educational Programs for Summer; Educational Programs for Winter, and Facilities, Structures, Activities, etc., that you DO NOT want in the Park.

The questionnaire recorded the age of the respondent, numbers in the household, and the area of the city in which the respondent lived. The content of the returns indicated that many families had sat down and discussed the questions before answering.

To prepare the public for the arrival of the questionnaire required special attention. Fears were expressed by conservationists that in completing the questionnaire, the public would not realize the type of land area that they were being asked to make suggestions for. This was a justifiable fear, as almost the entire land area was sealed off by private holdings. The public relations consultants obtained agreement of the *Calgary Herald* to publish a full-page photographic feature using three coloured photographs and a map. This ran the same day the questionnaires were distributed.

To stimulate the public response, the first news conference of Phase II was held after about 19,000 questionnaires had been tabulated. The

Canada's largest all-season urban park is now in the planning stages. With your help it can be the finest park of its kind in North America.

Fish Creek Park will eventually be three times as big as Vancouver's Stanley Park. At present, it is composed of natural vegetation and is largely free of development. It will reach all the way along Fish Creek from the Sarcee Reserve at 37th St. S.W. to the Bow River. That's a distance of six miles, averaging one-third mile in width.

What a wonderful opportunity for southern Albertans! The Alberta Government has asked a citizens' committee to seek public ideas before the Park is ever planned. This will ensure that this Park contributes to a parks system serving the widest possible cross section of citizens.

Excerpt from the questionnaire for the Park for All Seasons,
Francis, Williams & Johnson Ltd.

Honourable Dr. Allan Warrack, minister of forestry, and Bill Milne co-chaired the conference. Additional time was obtained on the broadcasting stations for committee members to report these trends.

Periodic news releases were issued, reporting on the returns and the trends the responses reflected. Advertising in Phase II concentrated on the questionnaire and stimulating a response by reporting on the returns and trends. Early in the project the committee had retained the services of the Lombard North Group Limited to produce a conceptual design based on the trends in the returns. They closely studied the returns in preparation for creation of the design concept.

On 22 April, after 29,000 of the 31,700 completed questionnaires had been received, the initial results were given to the media by the Advisory Committee. The results called for cross-country ski trails, bicycle trails, a swimming hole, and a ban on all-terrain vehicles, including snowmobiles.

Citizens responding urged some planned recreational areas and some undeveloped natural settings as well as the provision of outdoor cooking facilities and a winter skating rink. Special recreation areas for senior citizens and the handicapped were also recommended.

Phase III of the PR plan comprised presentation to the public of the Lombard North Group design, to culminate in a public hearing.

The public was informed from the beginning that even after their views from the questionnaire had been used to create a design concept, an opportunity would be provided to comment on the design. A news conference launched Phase III. Reporters were given the compilations of the questionnaire returns. A rendering of the design was displayed and a news kit provided. An in-depth briefing was given by the Lombard North Group on the design details. The media reaction to the news conference was positive.

Prior to the public hearing, the contour model of the park was redone to incorporate the concept design. It then was returned to the public library for display. CFAC-TV telecast its Fish Creek Park documentary the day before the hearing.

A news kit – containing the Lombard design, a fact sheet, and news release – was prepared for the hearing, and a special table provided for the reporters. Overrun copies from the newspapers of the park design were available to the public attending the hearing, held in the evening at the Jubilee Auditorium. A written invitation to attend the hearing was sent to each of the 192 organizations.

At the direction of Chairman Milne, the hearing, chaired by a Calgary lawyer, was informal. Every speaker complimented the committee on its work and, generally, on the design, although several had specific recommendations and comments concerning it.

As the PR plan execution neared its end, the mayor of Calgary, Rod Sykes, in a luncheon address, criticized the provincial government for taking a decision not to permit the construction of a six-lane freeway across the east end of the park. He charged the decision had been made without consulting the city and that the cost of alternate routs could soar to $15 million.

The provincial government had used the questionnaire returns in making its decision to prohibit the construction of the highway. The questionnaire trends and newspapers' letters-to-the-editor sections indicated public support of the provincial government's decision. The *Calgary Herald* also supported the decision:

> The provincial government's determination to prevent a six-lane, high-speed highway from passing through the new Fish Creek Provincial park sounds too obviously sensible to cause any controversy. The people of Calgary were asked what they wanted done with the park. Most of the 2,800 acres kept as natural as possible and the government agrees. The province is prepared to pay for the extra cost ... there is no place for a freeway running through Fish Creek Park.

The controversy ended quickly.

Today, residents of Calgary and southern Alberta and visitors are enjoying a unique park year-round. Located in the southern end of the city, it is a valley of 2,800 acres, approximately one-mile long and a mile and a half wide at its widest point. Its resident wildlife include deer, coyotes, blue herons, bald eagles, hawks, pelicans, owls, moles, weasels, and many beaver. There are no bears or cougars. They share their habitat with 1.5 million humans annually who skate and ski cross-country in winter; who cycle, hike, roller-blade skate, take guided walks, and swim the rest of the year. Also on site is an authentic ranch house that once was owned by Pat Burns, one of "the big four" who founded the Calgary Stampede.

Relations between the animals and visitors are good, although the flower beds of some homes bordering the park suffer from the deer who seem to prefer flowers to grass. Nobody said it was perfect.

CHAPTER 13

ALBERTA NURSES' STRIKE, 1977

S trikes are painful at any time. They are particularly so when they are by those who guard our health and safety. Some feel that specific categories of people serving the public, such as doctors, nurses, policemen, firemen, and civil servants, should not be permitted to strike. This opinion was expressed editorially by some newspapers at the conclusion of the 1977 nurses' strike in Alberta.

The right to strike is inherent in the process of labour negotiations. (A substitute for strike action that will satisfy both labour and management has not yet been discovered.) With its strengths and weaknesses, strike action continues to be a most important tool in the bargaining process.

The role of public relations during a strike is a vital one. Public opinion can bring strong pressure to bear on the union, on management, and on government. And the public that is well informed on both sides of the issue will come down on the side it is believed has a just policy and objective. It should be a major objective in every strike for each of the conflicting parties to fully and accurately inform its general and special publics of its objectives and the reasons for selecting them.

The PR principles, objectives, and planning described in the nurses' strike could have worked just as well for the nurses as it did for the Alberta Hospital Association (AHA), which retained the services of Francis, Williams & Johnson Ltd. (FWJ) to assist in the presentation of the AHA's position after negotiations with the Alberta Association of Registered Nurses (AARN) broke down in June 1977. The board of directors of the AHA represented 79 of Alberta's hospitals for bargaining.

The assignment for FWJ was to effectively present the AHA's position on the strike with a view to gaining public understanding and support for that position. To achieve that, I prepared a master plan.

This plan illustrates the details required for such a project. Foresight is of great importance, and lead time plays a significant role in the quality of the plan. In the strike, there were just a few days between the breakdown in negotiations and the walkout. But there was just enough time.

In addition to informing the general public about the AHA's stand, there were important special publics to inform. Hospital patients and their families were concerned about the prospects of a strike; doctors and nursing executives and supervisors wanted information, as did hospital employees who were not members of the nurses' union.

Prior to the walkout and after negotiations broke off, the master plan concentrated on development of media relations guidelines, and the selection of spokespersons and their preparedness to respond to questions from the media. Each hospital affected by the strike would need a spokesperson to respond to questions concerning negotiations after the walkout.

Three important policies were established early:

1. The welfare of the patients would continue to be the first priority of the hospitals and the AHA.
2. Only the AHA spokesman would issue information or respond to questions concerning the negotiations, while each hospital spokesperson would be responsible for the details of the hospital's emergency plan and the effect the strike was having on the hospital.
3. AHA and hospital spokespersons were advised to be factual and, above all, refrain from commenting on any personalities involved in the strike, either locally or provincially.

Work began on drafting a letter to patients concerning the strike vote. I then formulated 32 questions that were likely to be asked by journalists and worked with AHA staff officers to record, in writing, clear and accurate answers for each question. These were provided to the AHA spokesman, Verne Rheault, the AHA director of employee relations, and each hospital spokesperson.

The questions and answers formulated covered all of the strike issues. This aided hospital spokespersons, some of whom had only limited experience in working with the media. They ranged from the reason for a 6 percent wage increase offer by the AHA, to the role of the provincial government; from the rationale for the wage spread between the starting level for certified nursing aides and registered nurses – a strike issue – to the effects settlement at a higher level would have on hospitals.

Care was taken to avoid contentious language and unjustified or unfair criticism when preparing the answers. Following are six of the questions and answers from the list.

Q: **Why did negotiations break down and whose fault was it?**

A: Negotiations followed the normal and legal course of events. We feel our offer in conciliation of six percent was fair and equitable. The nurses, in turn, remained firm on their initial demand of 75 percent. After one-and-a-half days of conciliation talks, the conciliation officer recommended a strike or lockout, and the nurses applied for a strike vote.

Q: **Are you saying the nurses broke off negotiations?**

A: It was unfortunate that we could not agree but, yes, that is the case.

Q: **Don't you think the government has a responsibility to immediately legislate an end to this strike?**

A: That is a complex legal and to an extent moral and ethical question on which I do not feel competent to pass judgement. All actions by the nurses have been within the law.

Q: **Shouldn't doctors and nurses be forbidden to strike?**

A: Some feel strongly they should not be allowed to strike. But remember, the right to strike can be a good tool in the bargaining process if it is respected and not abused. We have seen the effects of an abused right to strike in Canada. Hopefully, we will never see such abuse in the health care field.

Q: **What has your experience been in dealing with the nurses as a bargaining unit?**

A: Nurses as individuals and as a group exhibit strong feelings of professionalism. They take great pride in their work and their service to the community. This is the first action of this type ever undertaken by nurses in Alberta.

Q: **What are the probable consequences of a long strike?**

A: The most apparent consequences of a long strike will be a

reduction in services to the community and possible complete
closure of some hospitals. Other consequences are difficult to pre-
dict. In any strike episode, the possibility of and the long-term
effects of any ill-feeling or high emotion arising from a strike is
too great to be ignored or taken lightly as a consequence.

During the period of the strike, all of the questions were posed and
answered. The accuracy and clarity of the responses by Rheault and the
hospital spokespersons were a major contribution towards assisting the
general public in obtaining a clearer picture of the AHA's and hospitals'
case.

Recognizing the fundamental importance of coordinated media relations before, during, and after the strike, we started work on a document
titled "Media Relations Guidelines." The questions and answers and the
above guidelines were presented to the AHA and the hospital administra-
tors at briefing seminars held in Edmonton and Calgary, chaired by the
AHA. Copies of the two documents were mailed to individuals unable to
attend.

The seminars proved valuable. There were never any contradictions
reported during the strike between the AHA spokesman and the spokespersons for the individual hospitals.

The media relations guidelines laid down four principles:

1.   Tell the truth.
2.   Give quick service.
3.   Don't ask favours.
4.   Respect deadlines.

The guidelines then expanded on these principles:

Tell the truth. It is not only good policy to tell the truth, it also is common sense. Dishonesty is always counterproductive. Revealing only half-
truths is the best way to ensure a story is only half-right, usually in your
worst interest.

In working with the media, be candid and cooperative. Be factual at
all times and avoid editorializing, i.e. stating opinions on facts or events of
which you are not 100 percent certain.

Give quick service. Listen carefully to a reporter's questions. Ask him or
her to repeat a question or rephrase it if you are unsure of its meaning.

Respond to each question with facts. Qualify any fact that may be unclear or any event still in transition by stating the situation is unclear or not resolved.

There is nothing wrong with saying, "I don't know the answer to that question." But you should also say, "I will find out the answer and be back to you immediately."

Find out the right answer and get back to the person with whom you spoke.

Such service shows honesty of effort and intent on your part. It is proof that you are prepared to cooperate.

Remember, if a reporter doesn't have your answer, he or she will do this story without it. Make sure your side of the story is in the story by responding quickly to requests.

Don't ask favours. Researching, interviewing, and producing interesting news stories are the job of the media professionals.

Respect the role and be forthright with them. Above all don't ask to see copy before it goes to press, and don't ask for a story to be killed or altered.

Such requests may even have the opposite effect of highlighting something you wish had been kept out.

Never discuss a subject "off the record." In truth *nothing* is "off the record," and your comment could be used if the reporter feels justified in doing so in the public interest.

Respect deadlines. The life of the media professional is governed by deadlines. Find out what type of deadline the reporters you meet are working towards. Ask them.

Help them meet that deadline by keeping your answers concise and your explanations brief but complete.

Get back to reporters quickly with requested information and offer to act as a further source of information or comment. Don't ask for extra time unless you absolutely require it, and make sure the reporter understands completely why you require it.

At the outset, the importance of the role of spokesperson was emphasized. The media relations guidelines, sent to all of the hospitals, suggested these recommendations concerning the selection of spokespersons:

Your spokesperson should possess these qualities:

1. an ability to listen and understand questions completely;
2. an ability to think and react coolly under pressure and in an uncomfortable environment (such as under harsh television lights);
3. an ability to answer questions with concise statements;
4. an even, well-modulated voice;
5. an ability to project honesty and sincere concern.

The job of spokesperson is a difficult one. Its importance should not be underestimated. Knowledge of the subject is a prerequisite.

Two additional projects contributed to disseminating the AHA's stance to the general and special publics: a factual history of the issues and events leading up to the strike, and a newspaper advertisement.

With a brief covering letter, the historical background paper was sent to all daily and weekly newspaper editors in Alberta and to news directors of radio and television stations.

It identified the strike's three major issues and then presented a table of salaries for prairie provinces and British Columbia of a nurse's first five years of employment. The table indicated that the 6 percent AHA offer placed Alberta nurses with slightly higher salaries than the other two Prairie provinces, but slightly lower than nurses in B.C. rates of pay for nursing aides and orderlies also were given, as were the differentials between registered nurses, and nursing aides and orderlies.

The AHA's position on the issue of control of standards of nursing care was explained. Management's view was that to undermine the authority of nursing management would produce a chaotic working environment, one which would not be in the best interest of patients.

The AHA's paper also contained a section titled "Impact of Nurses' Proposal." The section calculated that the proposed salary scale would increase the hourly cost of work by 36.84 percent. If the proposed reduction in hours worked was implemented, the hourly cost would increase by an additional 15.79 percent. The increase in the cost of an hour of work by a registered nurse due to the higher salary scale and the shorter work week which was proposed would have been 52.63 percent. If the requested increase in benefits had been granted, the increased costs would have been 21.54 percent.

If the AARN proposal had been implemented, the total increased cost to the employer for an hour of work performed by a registered nurse would have been estimated at 74.17 percent.

Probable costs of some of the other nurses' proposals would have been speculative, therefore the AHA projection did not include them. Among these were jury and witness leave, paid educational leave, additional Workers' Compensation Board benefits, and a bonus of $35 per trip when accompanying patients by ambulance.

The advertisement was placed in the daily and weekly newspapers after the issues appeared to become clouded, resulting in some confusion to the general public. The principles adhered to in producing the advertisement were: absolute accuracy, simplicity in wording, and design impact. It recorded the three main issues and, briefly and in simple language, stated the AHA's position on each.

The AHA entered the negotiations phase well prepared to present its position on the issues clearly and effectively. Two-way communication between the AHA in Edmonton and the hospitals scattered across the province was established and maintained. The hospital spokespersons were kept informed of AHA statements to the media. They were confined to providing information to the media on their hospital's contingency plan and the effect of the strike on the hospital. They did not comment on negotiations – nor could they with any certainty of accuracy. Thus, no contradictions arose between the AHA and the hospitals. The information being disseminated from both sources was accurate, and confusion about issues was avoided.

Early in the strike a serious potential problem arose. The AHA's legal counsel advised the association not to comment to the media. I discussed this advice with the AHA management, telling them that silence would result in disaster and their best course of action was to tell the truth accurately and quickly. After the strike, the legal counsel graciously wrote a letter to the AHA saying the decision to keep the media informed was the right one.

The public had supported the AHA's position and the strike ended with government intervention ordering the nurses back to work. The PR plan's objectives had been achieved. There was no significant public reaction against the decision.

CHAPTER 14

CANMORE MINES

In the spring of 1979, a management crisis arose for the Dillingham Corporation of Canada when a decision was taken to suspend operations indefinitely of its mine at Canmore, Alberta. A coal producer, Canmore Mines had begun operations in 1890. The affected employees included 108 miners, whose average age was 46, and 32 staff members.

Dillingham was the first Canadian producer to sell coal to the Japanese. The mine had been closed down many times in the past, the most recent occasion being a partial closure, from June to October 1972, because of a slump caused by low-cost plentiful petroleum coke, a shift to liquid natural gas, and an increased number of electric furnaces.

Canmore Mines had lost money for seven of the last nine years. Its coal had limited application; it was used primarily for mixing with other coals in industrial applications. It had but one customer, a Japanese consortium. Potential customers were restricted in number and it was impossible to increase production to a point where the mine was economically justifiable. The worldwide recession of 1975 brought on a slump and sales continued to decline.

Canmore coal had been priced out of the market. A 109 percent increase in freight rates to Eastern Canada within one year aborted an effort to sell coal to chemical companies there.

About mid-June, Dillingham retained the services of Francis, Williams & Johnson Ltd. (FWJ). I was assigned to the project, the objective of which was to produce a PR plan to effectively communicate the corporation's position to its special publics (including employees) and the general public, with a view to minimizing damage to all parties, in particular Canmore Mines and Dillingham Corporation of Canada.

The plan indicated media interest would be broad and include media of Canmore, Calgary, and the province of Alberta, with some national interest throughout Canada. It also anticipated interest from Canadian trade and financial publications, as well as the United States, Dow Jones, and Reuters. This widely spread interest was anticipated because job losses are a politically sensitive subject, and Canmore was in the federal riding of Prime Minister Joe Clark. Not only would the government be interested, so would the government opposition. In addition, Dillingham of Canada's parent company was American, with head offices located in Honolulu. Our past experience was that labour/management issues generated heated struggles between the contestants.

The plan identified three categories of special publics: politicians at the three levels of government; three levels of appointed government officials; and business associates, union leaders and all employees. Added to these was the general public.

Questions to be answered included why the mine was closing, what impact it would have on the employees and the community, and what the corporation planned to do for its employees. Several information vehicles were chosen to disseminate key information.

When our company's services were retained, a final decision concerning closure was not planned until a corporate board meeting to be held on 25 June in Vancouver. This gave us approximately 10 days to plan the means of information, including briefings for the Alberta government and the elected and appointed officials of Canmore.

All members of the briefing team were senior executives from the mine. Heading the team was Charles W. Gregory, executive vice-president and general manager. Anticipated questions and their answers were developed for the use of those involved in the briefings. A total of 42 questions were formulated and, with the help of management, answers were prepared. Five of the questions are listed below:

> **Can't your company demonstrate compassion for its older employees having long service? Couldn't you put enough aside to take care of 22 miners already in their 50's?**

> **Would you keep the mine in operation if government provided a subsidy?**

> How Canadian is Dillingham Corporation of Canada?
> Who made the decision to close the mine – which cor-
> poration?
>
> Rising freight rates has been a major cause of your
> inability to make Canmore Mines economically viable.
> Wouldn't you agree therefore that the federal govern-
> ment played a major role in putting you and your
> employees out of business? The federal government sets
> the freight rates – not the provincial government.
>
> How many children 18 years of age and under are
> affected? [Better to know the answer. To not know may
> be perceived as callousness.]

A news release was prepared which outlined the Dillingham position.
It incorporated the reasons why they were shutting Canmore Mines, with
quotes attributed to Charles Gregory. He would represent management at
the news conference. If questions during the briefings, the news conference, or from individuals did not prompt the following response, Gregory
would introduce it:

> Only after individual consultations will the answers of
> the employment question be known. However, I can tell
> you we are or will be:
>
> a)   Researching available alternative work.
> b)   Notifying other mines by providing résumés.
> c)   Researching government services.
> d)   Interviewing and counselling each employee.
> e)   Developing a plan for each employee.
> f)   Where required, linking spouse or family into the
>   planning.
> g)   Where possible, assisting in initiation and imple-
>   mentation of each plan.

A fact sheet was produced for handout which contained briefly the
corporation's Canadian operations, its locations, names and positions of
Gregory and R.J. Meyers of Vancouver, B.C. (president of Dillingham
Corporation Canada Ltd.); when operations would be suspended, i.e.,

July 13, 1979; why the mine was being closed and the termination provisions covering pensions, severance pay, and holidays.

Two documents were produced to ensure coordination of the PR plan: A schedule of events for the corporation – with copies to the Canadian corporate headquarters in Honolulu, the vice-president and general manager of Canmore Mines – and the schedule of events for FWJ's PR department, which was given the same distribution.

The decision to close the mine was made 25 June at a board meeting in Vancouver. During this crucial period, the following actions took place:

June 25: The decision was received by FWJ from the board. The board was alerted to the significance of the Tokyo Economic Summit Conference 28–29 June. Prime Minister Clark is likely to be accompanied by the minister of Industry Trade and Commerce and the minister of EMR. Canmore is the prime minister's constituency. FWJ and Dillingham executives formulated answers to anticipated questions.

June 26: The draft PR plan, news release fact sheet, and distribution list were reviewed for possible amendments. Only minor changes were needed. FWJ produced the necessary copies. The briefing team, after consideration, determined their requirements. These, too, were produced by FWJ's PR department. The mine's management obtained briefing appointments for elected and appointed officials in Calgary and Edmonton for 28 June.

June 28: Alberta's ministers of Energy and Natural Resources and Labour were briefed in Edmonton at 9 a.m. At 11 a.m., the director of the Mines Branch of the Department of Labour was briefed. The briefing team arrived in Calgary from Edmonton at 2 p.m. At 2:30 p.m. representatives from the Energy Resources Conservation Board were briefed. Following these briefings, I was provided with information regarding what had taken place.

June 29: The president of the union and the mayor of Canmore were briefed in Canmore at 9 a.m. An hour later in Calgary distribution of the news release began. Simultaneously, the mine manager had the release delivered to the media in Canmore and nearby Banff. At 10:30 a.m., the mine president briefed staff supervisors in Canmore. From 10:30 a.m. to noon, the mine's executive vice-president, in the presence of the union president, briefed the union's local officers. I had positioned an FWJ account manager at Canmore Mines at 8 a.m. to carry out media functions and keep the PR department in Calgary informed.

He also informed Dillingham Corporation in Vancouver that the news release had been delivered while ensuring that the Vancouver spokesperson had all the necessary background to respond to media enquiries. He then telexed Dillingham, Vancouver, that the release had been made.

The same day, in the PR office in Calgary, a pre-punched telex, on notification from Canmore, transmitted the release to Hon. R. Hnyatyshyn, minister of Energy, Mines and Resources, and R.P. Mullvihill, Department of Industry, Trade and Commerce, Ottawa. They were informed that the release had been given to the Calgary media that day. The same release was sent to the prime minister's office in Ottawa, also informing them that the release had been sent to the Canadian Ambassador in Tokyo, adding that since Canmore was Prime Minister Clark's constituency, the information might be helpful. Identical information was passed on to the Canadian Ambassador in Tokyo, with the suggestion that reporters accompanying the prime minister might submit questions.

Commencing 30 June the PR department monitored the local (Calgary), provincial, and national media. Mine management monitored Canmore-Banff newspapers and the Canmore community. Findings from both locations were provided to the Dillingham offices in both Honolulu and Vancouver.

For about two weeks after the Canmore news conference (immediately after the release was distributed, reporters moved into the Canmore community anticipating a news break), individual reporters were granted interviews by the executive vice-president. They also interviewed the miners and staff, union leaders, and the town's mayor. Representatives of provincial opposition parties also interviewed Canmore residents.

There were no criticisms of Canmore Mines' management, nor Dillingham Corporation. The corporation's labour relations had been sound in the past, and the executive vice-president was well respected by the union's leaders and its members. He was also knowledgeable.

Union leaders cooperated and refrained from criticism of management. There were no criticisms from elected politicians of any party at any level. Governing politicians expressed gratitude for the "timely" briefings.

The only criticism was about freight rates, directed at the Canadian Pacific Railway. One publication dealt with their impact on Western Canada.

The project had presented neither serious problems, nor unexpected incidents – except for the freight rate criticism. It did, however, require detailed planning and some hard work. I believe that the union and corporate executives were primarily responsible for what was achieved. The PR department's major contribution was the preparation of accurate information and keeping all parties informed as quickly as possible.

Canmore recovered from the loss of the mine. Today it is a thriving tourist destination, boasting the Nordic skiing facilities from the 1988 Winter Olympic Games and several golf courses.

CHAPTER 15

PUBLIC RELATIONS AND THE ABUSE OF POLITICAL POWER

The conflict between the federal government and Alberta over the taxing of gas and oil revenues began before Premier Peter Lougheed came to power in 1971. But he brought the conflict to a head in September of that same year when he took control of provincial resources and adjusted Alberta's share of oil and gas royalties. He also moved towards slowing gas exports until the wellhead price reflected a fairer market value.

In 1972 he began transferring price control of oil and gas from the multinational oil and gas companies to the people of Alberta, who owned the resources.

On 3 September 1973, the federal government instituted a Federal Export Oil Tax. Prime Minister Trudeau's action infuriated Lougheed. He charged it was the "most discriminatory action taken by a federal government against a particular province in the history of Confederation." He demanded to know why the tax hadn't been imposed on Saskatchewan potash, B.C. lumber, and asbestos and gold from Quebec and Ontario.

Trudeau said the federal government's objective was to balance regional and national growth and development, and he was concerned Alberta's royalties from oil and gas would diminish the federal government's potential income from corporate taxation. He charged these royalties were eroding the corporate tax base, and he threatened any action taken by Lougheed in respect of royalties "would have to be without prejudice to our freedom of action as regards federal taxation." Lougheed believed Trudeau was thinking about taxing Alberta's royalties.

Among other points of friction were Ontario Premier William Davis's proposed policy that his province should have as much right in the setting of oil and gas prices as the federal government. Davis wanted to shut down Alberta's Heritage Fund and transfer the money to the federal treasury.

Another cause of friction was the Trudeau government's purchase of Mexican oil at world price, while paying 40 percent less for Alberta oil.

On 28 October 1980, the National Energy Program (NEP) was announced as part of the federal government budget. The NEP back-in clause, whereby Petro-Canada, without contribution or effort, would take over 25 percent of the value of any company's exploration and production on federal lands, only added fuel to the conflict. The Hon. Marc Lalonde, minister of Energy, Mines and Resources, had declared that the NEP had been created to Canadianize the industry and to help the country's oil and gas companies.

The oil industry has two associations: the Independent Petroleum Association of Canada (IPAC), made up of the smaller Canadian oil and gas companies, and the Canadian Petroleum Association (CPA), whose members include the large international companies, as well as some of the larger independent Canadian companies. IPAC not only disagreed with the minister's view that the NEP would help their members, they believed strongly that the program would cause irreparable damage to the companies Lalonde claimed it would benefit. IPAC believed the NEP would adversely affect their cash flow and threaten the ownership of the business of member companies. They believed the NEP would drive them out of Canada to explore for oil in the United States, where investment returns were much higher. They foresaw thousands of jobs in and outside of Canada's oil industry being lost and Canadians having greater dependency on high-cost foreign crude. They also feared Canada would lose the opportunity to achieve oil self-sufficiency.

Late in October 1980, IPAC retained the services of Francis, Williams & Johnson Ltd., public relations and advertising counsel, to assist the association in making the bold move of taking their case to the Canadian public. John Francis and I, with support staff, began the planning.

Four surveys and 1979–80 newspaper clippings on the industry were studied in preparation for drafting the IPAC public relations plan. The surveys included one conducted in 1979 for the Petroleum Resources Communication Foundation in the city of London, Ontario, and three surveys and a supplementary report conducted Canada-wide in 1979 and 1980 for the same organization.

The surveys indicated Canadians generally supported government intervention in the gas and oil industry. Also, a small majority supported the policy of lower gas and oil prices. The weight of the support was concentrated in the voting population of central Canada.

Support for the industry was confined to Alberta and parts of the resource provinces, primarily B.C. and Saskatchewan. The petroleum industry was not a popular one in the minds of most Canadians.

The objective of the plan was "to keep the contentious issues and IPAC's stance on the energy program and budget before the general and special publics until such a time as the federal government implements satisfactory remedial amendments."

In addition to the general public, the following special publics were targeted: members of the federal Parliament; members of the legislative and national assemblies; members of the oil and gas industry, including employees and their families; suppliers to the oil and gas industry; and military organizations. While all of the plan's programs reached out to Canadians from coast-to-coast, a special concentration of effort was made in Ontario and Quebec. The media in Ottawa and members of Parliament were priority targets.

The message of the PR plan was simple: to show the adverse impact the NEP would have on Canadians everywhere, not just in the West; the need for higher prices; the impact of job cutbacks in all parts of Canada; and the importance of self-sufficiency in oil and gas, i.e., the danger of relying on foreign supply.

Essentially, the strategy unveiled by research was to tell Canadians that the NEP would hurt them, explain how, then encourage them to speak to their members of Parliament, who would in turn urge the government policymakers to modify the program.

Two telephone surveys were conducted: one, two weeks before the plan was conducted; and the other, two weeks after it was launched. Samples of 50 respondents in each of Vancouver, Calgary, Toronto, Ottawa, Montreal, and Halifax were contacted. The sample size provided evidence of shifts in public opinion and differences between cities.

The plan included advertising and print and electronic interviews in 13 major cities by Calgary executives of IPAC positioned in the 13 locations when the plan was launched. All of the executives were given training in media interviews and provided with a well-researched document incorporating industry opposition to the NEP and the reasons why. They would emphasize that a large number of the companies objecting to the NEP were Canadian companies; They would also recommend that the NEP be withdrawn or amended.

The material provided to the potential spokesmen also included specific examples of ways in which costs were rising and the ways in which NEP would reduce incentive and revenues. Examples also were given of the higher revenue and lower costs in the United States and of the number of Canadian companies affected and the dollars they were diverting to the U.S.

The IPAC public relations plan was launched with a full-page advertisement being published in daily newspapers where spokesmen were positioned. And it focused on the minister of Energy, Mines and Resources. Here is what it said:

MR. LALONDE

YOUR ENERGY POLICY WILL HARM CANADIANS

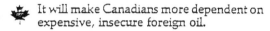 It will make Canadians more dependent on expensive, insecure foreign oil.

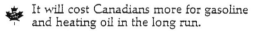 It will cost Canadians more for gasoline and heating oil in the long run.

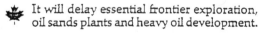 It will delay essential frontier exploration, oil sands plants and heavy oil development.

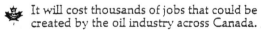 It will cost thousands of jobs that could be created by the oil industry across Canada.

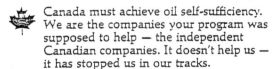 Canada must achieve oil self-sufficiency. We are the companies your program was supposed to help — the independent Canadian companies. It doesn't help us — it has stopped us in our tracks.

We urge you to reconsider this program for the good of all Canadians.

INDEPENDENT PETROLEUM ASSOCIATION OF CANADA

IPAC is the voice of the Canadian-owned petroleum companies.
Two hundred members are oil and gas exploration companies.
One hundred and forty additional members provide essential services to
the Canadian petroleum industry.

Before the plan was implemented, FWJ involved its own associate companies of Inside Canada Public Relations (now WORLDCOM). Their purpose was to assist the IPAC spokesmen to obtain interviews. The spokesmen were positioned in St. John's, Halifax, Montreal, Ottawa, Toronto, Regina, Saskatoon, Edmonton, Calgary, and Vancouver the day the ad was published.

The day the ad appeared, and for about three days thereafter, the spokesmen, through newspaper, radio, and television, presented Canadians from coast-to-coast with a detailed follow-up that expressed the fears and convictions of IPAC members. For example, in St. John's, Newfoundland, IPAC spokesman George Wahl received coverage in both of the city's daily newspapers that also covered the province. He spent two hours and 15 minutes conducting radio interviews and 40 minutes doing television interviews.

A Canadian Press story, based on a one-hour interview with spokesman Ron Coleman, went to all media in Nova Scotia, New Brunswick, and Prince Edward Island. In addition, Coleman received extensive coverage in the Halifax dailies and was interviewed by telephone by the *Cape Breton Post, Saint John Telegraph-Journal*, and the *Daily Gleaner* of Fredericton. He also was interviewed for 10 minutes for the CBC morning show, 12 minutes for CJCH-TV, and did a 30-minute interview on CBH-TV.

In Ontario, IPAC spokesman Rick Harrop gave a total of 30 print and broadcast interviews, covering Toronto, Hamilton, Kitchener-Waterloo, Guelph, and London.

With the exception of two cities – Montreal and Calgary – the IPAC spokesmen's activities and coverage were similar to those of the Maritimes and Ontario. Only three interviews were given by spokesman Ronald White in Montreal, a one-hour interview with Jacques Forget of the weekly publication *Finance*, an eight-minute CBC radio "Daybreak" telephone interview, and an interview with Jean-Paul Gagné of "Journal Les Affaires." Mr. White was unilingual and before his arrival in Montreal, IPAC had tried to identify a French-speaking member within its association who could travel to Quebec. The search failed and before Mr. White reached Montreal the story broke in Toronto, Ottawa, and London. However, the Quebec media did receive those stories from Canadian Press and other agencies.

The Calgary problem was of a different nature. In Alberta, IPAC adopted a responsive rather than an aggressive approach to the media. Since the country's major source of gas and oil is in their province, the Alberta media were well informed on the industry. They already were closely following the NEP conflict between the Alberta and federal governments. It would have been presumptuous of IPAC to request that the Alberta media do interviews with the spokesman based on the ad. Still, coverage in Alberta did not suffer.

Early on the morning of 17 November, the Alberta media began receiving the wire service stories breaking in the East. And IPAC received extensive space and time in the Alberta media. IPAC headquarters in Calgary received 30 media telephone calls that day, not only from journalists in Eastern Canada, but also in Calgary and Edmonton.

A spin-off from the spokesmen's activities was the personal contact IPAC members made with journalists across the country. The journalists located outside of Alberta had met individuals knowledgeable about the oil and gas industry that they could approach with ease.

The print media stories were nearly unanimous across Canada in reporting and supporting the IPAC campaign. Following are a few excerpts.

Southam's economic editor Don McGillivray's column appeared in the newspaper chain's dailies in the East and West under an Ottawa dateline. It read:

> If Alberta was Saudi Arabia, Pierre Trudeau would have arrived in Edmonton with half a ton of gifts and six-year-old Sacha dressed in cowboy costume in an attempt to charm his hosts by paying a compliment to their culture. But Alberta isn't Saudi Arabia, even though the constitution – as it used to be interpreted – gives the province about the same control of its resources as the desert kingdom has.
>
> So instead of trying to sweet-talk Alberta out of its oil at the price set by Albertans, the federal government is in effect seizing the oil and unilaterally setting the price far below what Trudeau would gladly pay to Saudi Arabia.
>
> The harsh words are reserved for Canadians who happen to live in the West. The smooth diplomacy is for export only.

David Todd of the Vancouver *Province* reported under a Victoria dateline that the Canadian Petroleum Association's B.C. chairman, Eric Connor, was unhappy with the NEP.

> The federal government's proposed eight percent tax on oil and natural gas production will reduce corporate profit levels for some B.C. companies by as much as 50 percent next year, a spokesman for the Canadian Petroleum Association charged Monday.

> Eric Connor, the CPA's B.C. chairman, said the Trudeau government's new tax will also reduce after-tax income from Alberta crude oil by 21 percent and put production from most Saskatchewan fields in the red.

Tracey LeMay of the *Ottawa Citizen* interviewed Earl Joudrie, president of IPAC and chief executive officer of Calgary-based Voyager Petroleums Ltd.

> The program, which formed the major part of last month's federal budget, inhibits oil exploration by Canadian firms and, as a result, means that the country will never become energy self-sufficient, Joudrie maintains.

> It will mean equipment and personnel will be going to the U.S., he adds.

A month later, in December, Minister Lalonde replied that the NEP had been fully considered and the criticisms were "unwarranted." A reply by IPAC held firmly to its views. Later in January, Richard Thomson, chairman of the Toronto Dominion Bank, was reported in the Toronto *Globe and Mail* as having told the bank's annual meeting that the federal government's National Energy Program could produce a "national disaster."

Describing the PR results achieved, the FWJ report stated:

> Unlike most programs of this kind where clippings and an interview count is used as the measure of results, in this particular case a far more scientific technique was used.

> A professional survey company ... was retained to conduct surveys before and after the national program ... there is ample evidence of dramatic changes in the public

understanding from one week to the next. And these changes occurred in most of the cities surveyed. These were shifts in favour of the petroleum industry. The most significant occurred in Ottawa.

... it should be noted that the advertisement and the interviews did not deal so much with asking the public to establish a position or change an attitude, but rather with information.

The greatest compliments came from the three leading politicians from opposing sides. Premier Peter Lougheed said that the program was tremendously effective. Senator Keith Davey said the program was the most effective single thing that had been done. He specifically referred to the fact that although the NEP had masses of support, everywhere the government turned it ran into the question, "But why are you hurting the Canadian companies?" Honourable Marc Lalonde promised to meet with the industry and has done so on frequent occasions. He has modified his program to some degree, but not sufficiently for the industry as yet.

In the case of Ottawa, in the response to the question "Are you in favour of the new federal energy policy which was announced last October 28?", only 23 percent were opposed before IPAC implemented its PR plan. The opposition jumped to 42 percent in the survey done after the plan was launched.

The report summarized results in the surveyed cities as follows:

- The direction of movement within the survey week was generally towards the IPAC position.
- Vancouver and Calgary were the only two cities indicating majority opposition to the federal energy policy.
- Gains in attitude towards the IPAC position were evident in Ottawa.
- Some gains in attitude were evident in Toronto, but some results moved in a negative direction.
- Attitudes in Halifax were more negative, away from the IPAC position, between the first and second week of the survey.

- The credibility of the oil and gas industry was seen to increase in Vancouver. Minor shifts occurred in the other cities.

As a result of the PR plan, millions of Canadians had been informed of the problems they would face as a result of the NEP. Many journalists, print and broadcast, had acquired greatly expanded knowledge of the oil and gas industry, and majority opinion, while in favour of the NEP, had begun to shift towards the petroleum industry.

In 1984, when the Mulroney government came to power, every Alberta seat was occupied by a Conservative. They had promised to repeal the NEP. But for three years after coming to power, they continued to drain income from Alberta's major industry. This failure to fulfil a promise, as well as the awarding of a major contract for fighter aircraft to Quebec, resulted in the birth of the Reform Party of Canada in 1987.

I had been working in the private sector for six years before the NEP was launched and had "picked up the form." I was comfortable working with the IPAC executives.

Some amendments to the plan were made within the first year, but the plan's objective was not fully achieved until seven years after its implementation. While success was only partial, the plan did begin the process of shifting public opinion outside of Alberta closer to the oil and gas industry's side of the issue. Before the NEP, public opinion outside of Alberta was strongly influenced against the province and its major industry by two factors: the Heritage Trust Fund and an automobile bumper sticker.

Lougheed introduced the Heritage Trust Fund in the spring of 1975. Oil and gas revenues would be placed in the fund as "an investment for the future." A significant portion would be invested in a manner which reflected the "claim of young Albertans and Albertans not yet born." Such investments, Lougheed said, must be made "with a minimum of interference in the competitive private sector," including financial institutions. He believed the bulk of the investments should be made in Alberta and "acceptable generally to Albertans."

From Albertans' points of view, the revenues from the non-renewable resources were an investment in their future. Ontario and Quebec had their hydro-electric companies. Still, the Heritage Fund created envy in Canada's other provinces.

The bumper sticker incident, at least six years prior to the NEP, has never been fully explained. A Canadian Press wire photo showing an

Alberta bumper sticker proclaiming "Let the Eastern Bastards Freeze in the Dark" was published in newspapers from coast-to-coast. It is said 500 were produced and 20 appeared on Alberta automobiles. I never saw even one of the 20, and I've never heard who ordered them to be produced.

The impact of these two factors, combined with the boom Alberta was experiencing from an overheated economy, turned public opinion against the province – opinion which we helped to shift.

CHAPTER 16

A LOOK BENEATH THE BOTTOM LINE

AUTHOR'S NOTE: In the preface, I expressed the hope that this book would prove helpful to corporate and government executives, PR practitioners, and PR students seeking to expand their knowledge of the public relations function. The previous chapter provided background relating to John Francis. It is a background that combines considerable depth, both in PR and in business. As national president (1989–90) of the Canadian Public Relations Society (CPRS), he expressed views particularly relevant to corporations and government, PR practitioners, students, and lawyers. I invited him to incorporate changes in the message which would reflect current thinking in this rapidly evolving field. His views also reflect the ethical standards of CPRS. Here is what he wrote.

Business and government have reached a crossroads in the way they deal with public opinion. Every day we see evidence that the public is no longer satisfied with assurances that business is looking after things and the government is regulating those that don't. The public has now found ways to take action of its own.

The public relations profession has a crucial role to play in this new order that will confront society in the 1990s.

Below are some examples from the business world that demonstrate why business will need to work much harder in public relations in the future. The government's future role in public communication is also examined. There are a number of important roles for public relations professionals in this communications society.

First, let me define what I mean by "Beneath the Bottom Line." The performance of corporations is measured by the bottom line, or earnings-per-share in a quarter or year. What is beneath the bottom line of every corporation is the financial risk it creates during a current quarter which may materialize in the next quarter or the next decade; for instance, production of faulty products, environmental damage, pollution, unsafe working environments, executive crime, and misleading advertising, to name a few. We've seen them all in the last few years. The costs to the companies and governments involved have been horrendous. They take the form of additional health care costs, clean-ups, jail sentences, class-action law suits, and labour disruptions. For my definition, these costs are beneath the bottom line until they are realized; then they move above the line where they cut into profits. Business is traditionally guided by the bottom line. Business schools teach the bottom line as the ultimate goal. Financial markets reward the bottom line. Even governments need a good bottom line from business in order to collect more taxes. I am a free enterpriser and I support this system. However, business has backed itself into a corner in recent years.

Let us begin with the Exxon *Valdez* oil tanker spill. This was a case of a company listening to its broker and its lawyer, instead of listening to its public relations advisors and the general public. Exxon's responses were laced with reference to the minimal impact on the bottom line (to reassure the financial markets), and their efforts to minimize the company's legal liability. Neither of these strategies succeeded, as the company was forced to spend more and more money and to defend itself in a number of lawsuits, which resulted in large financial settlements. Some loss of public trust and goodwill is permanent. A *Fortune* magazine poll of corporate executives, directors, and financial analysts revealed that Exxon has fallen from number six to number 110 among the most admired U.S. corporations. It is interesting to note that a corporation giving to environmental causes has doubled since Exxon *Valdez*, a clear demonstration that this event was a major turning point in corporate attitudes about the environment.

Further evidence of growing public concern is demonstrated by a survey of small business executives by Arthur Anderson & Co., which indicated that 73 percent of executives of small business favour tougher action against polluters.

Now let's move over to the food business, where Kraft Foods Limited made a mistake in a contest entry form. Instead of offering one van as a prize, they somehow offered 100. Their immediate reaction was to pull in their horns, probably with legal advice, and to admit no liability. Instant negative publicity occurred. It would have cost Kraft $1.7 million to give away 100 vans; the positive publicity would have been fantastic. In fact, it would have been worth far more than $1.7 million spent on television advertising. Instead they chose evasion and denial, lost the public opinion battle in the first two days, and faced class-action suits which probably cost them as much in legal fees as a customer-sensitive settlement would have cost.

Still another area of public concern about social responsibility is demonstrated by the reaction of the business world to AIDS, drugs, and alcohol. Many business people react to the AIDS threat with the comment, "Let them die." This not only reflects a lack of understanding of the disease – and a head-in-the-sand attitude about society – it demonstrates an ignorance about what AIDS will cost business, both directly and indirectly, through health care taxation over the next two decades. AIDS carries a massive cost and we will all pay for it. A similar analogy can be made with drugs and alcohol. Too frequently business keeps its head down, hoping someone else solves the problem. There seems to be a reluctance on the part of business to deal with their own cases and to pay for the overall social cost of treatment and education. Yet business pays the price through lost productivity, or worse.

The inadequate business response to the waste management crisis and a sluggishness in withdrawing chemicals which damage the environment are further examples. We need not look far afield for evidence of damage. The Three-Mile Island nuclear disaster, virtually indestructible PCBs, Marathon Oil and its fluoride problem at Texas City, our disintegrating ozone layer, and global warming ought to make the business world take notice.

Transportation is an important area for public responsibility and public relations. Companies, governments, and unions which move people and goods are going to require better management, better technicians, better educated people, better recruitment, and better training. Think about the hazards. Transporters need to understand chemicals, terrorists, accidents, mob behaviour, sickness, rescue systems, the laws of liability, and how the news media operate.

Watch for insurance companies to wake up to their responsibility in accident prevention and health safety issues. This is long overdue.

My thesis is that many businesses are so driven by the bottom line today, they have difficulty looking beyond the quarterly results. I was interested to note that Prime Minister Brian Mulroney made reference to the need for business to look further than the quarterly results in a public speech. That is a signal from government. In another speech, the prime minister told the energy industry to put environmental protection at the top of its agenda, warning, "We are going to strengthen our environmental assessment review process in further legislation."

John Paluszek, past president of the Public Relations Society of America, wrote a paper entitled "Social Capitalism in the Noisy 1990s." For an American, even that title is a swing from the far right. He identified an agenda of social problems that business and its communicators will need to deal with and the new needs of the working class, including parental leave and daycare, the political muscle of an aging population, the political and corporate dynamite of environmental issues, the world's most litigious society, and the tragedy of the permanent underclass. His central hypothesis was this: "Privately-owned American business has become an instrument of public will in ameliorating many social problems."

There are two obvious causes of the inadequate response from business. One is the legal system in the United States, which encourages ridiculously high settlements. At the bottom of this is contingency fees for lawyers. Companies fear huge settlements, particularly huge class-action settlements and, therefore, go into a shell rather than deal with their problems in an open, honest way. We have similar problems in Canada, although not as powerful.

The other problem is corporate takeovers. Driven by the bottom line, the financial community in the '80s created the junk bond phenomenon and a fantastic drive for power and wealth. This process contributed nothing positive to society. How can a corporate chairman, who is beleaguered by the fear of a takeover, deal effectively with the necessary planning and investment required to be a responsible corporate citizen? And what about the winners of these takeover battles – can we expect them to invest beneath the bottom line?

Governments in Canada and the United States are showing a serious interest in these major challenges. With the public genuinely concerned about the environment – and people like David Suzuki warning us that we have 10 years to save our planet – the government has the voter on its side for the first time on the environmental issue; other issues, such as AIDS and drugs, are not far behind.

Over recent decades, governments have mostly rattled sabres at business. But there's evidence that direct government intervention will increase, an idea the public supports. This means governments will be making new laws, providing systems of enforcement, and strengthening both civil and criminal penalties.

Historically, the government of Canada has responded to a small oligarchy of business and union leaders who had direct access to the prime minister's office. This is no longer true. Our governments, federal and provincial, are demonstrating a readiness to be independent of powerful lobbies and the influence of large campaign donations.

Recent examples include the federal government's environmental initiative to intervene in provincial plans for pulp mills in Alberta and water development in Saskatchewan. The provinces want to create jobs, but the federal government is focusing on environmental protection.

The government will be much more actively involved with business in the 1990s. A whole new infrastructure of consultation is developing, where people with common concerns meet at the table and formulate plans to prevent crisis. This applies particularly in the environmental field. But regulation of environmental damage, such as pollution, is an extremely complicated process.

A study paper by the Law Reform Commission of Canada demonstrates that using legal methods and including penalties to regulate pollution is a quagmire of interpretations. Because of the difficulties of interpreting and defining the nature of pollution, government has found in recent years that much more can be accomplished through informal contact than through prosecution. We can extend these difficulties to other forms of environmental damage. The Law Reform Commission study paper identifies trends in pollution control. They include increased public participation and increasing use of prosecutions and enforcement squads. Governments are also using financial incentives rather than coercive measures to get quicker and more effective environmental protection.

Remedies, Processes, and Techniques

Wherever you have more discussion and less enforcement, people with public relations skills and experience will be given the freedom and encouragement to try for remedies. Obviously *the public participation process* is one of the pre-eminent means of protection through planning, as distinct from protection through penalty. Recent trends in public participation demonstrate a much greater sincerity on the part of all participants than was the case in the past. We all recall the battle between the Sierra

Club and the U.S. Army Corps of Engineers when the preservation of the tiny snail darter held up construction of a water project. That seemed to be an extreme. Today we have ordinary citizens sitting at the table with the company and the government in public forums and private sessions to discuss the detailed implications of development plans.

Companies are finding that citizens have good ideas and solutions to problems and are not exclusively bent on blocking plans. Facilitating these kinds of discussions is part of the public relations process. It depends on the principles followed by PR professionals. These include a requirement for two-way communication, a clear understanding of what all parties are thinking and saying, and creating means to bring them closer together.

The purchase of media to explain policies and programs is another trend for the future. We have seen television networks fight off corporate and government information programs, while at the same time filling the airwaves with trash. In future, all parties are going to understand better the boundaries on the difference between advocacy and information. They will discover that information programs which are honest and complete will be of greater value than so-called advocacy programming, which sometimes tells only half the story.

Newspapers are always open to companies and governments that have information to pass along in the form of paid space. We get into semantic traps here too frequently. Because this is purchased through the advertising department it is called "advertising," but most often it is simply information with a box around it. When we call it advertising, chief executives and politicians equate it with the product advertising they see on a daily basis. They then conclude that they do not want their company or government to be tarnished by association and therefore they miss out on the very best means of communication available to them. The best single means of mass distribution of a package of information is simply to buy the space and put the information in it, whether it is newspaper, radio, television, or magazine. Why is this effective? Because it is complete; that is, all the necessary information can be delivered at the same time. It is controlled, meaning reporters cannot interfere with the order or the emphasis. It is creative – language and pictures and graphic illustration can be used to clarify the information. It reaches the chosen audience by virtue of the fact that space and time can be purchased in the mass media appropriately targeted to varying audiences. And most important of all, it can be repeated. Repetition is necessary when messages are complicated. No other means of public communication comes anywhere near this in achieving communications objectives in the public arena.

The 1988 Free Trade communications battle in Canada will stand as a landmark event. It demonstrated the best and worst in the usage of paid space. The worst was obviously the extremely misleading emotional treatment used by the NDP in television advertising, and the best was the informative program by the Business Alliance for Job Opportunities.

Still another strategy of the public relations professional is *crisis management*. This incorporates both planning for the crisis and reacting to it. More and more, executives are being trained by public relations professionals in how to deal with a crisis, recognizing that the first few hours of a crisis determine the public's ultimate view of who is at fault and who should be punished or blamed. Historically, the people responsible have tended to be secretive, uncooperative, and apprehensive about dealing with the public in a crisis situation. This is changing and the preparation of plans for crisis is penetrating the industrial world. The upside is that large responsible companies are implementing these programs. The downside is that generally smaller and often irresponsible companies aren't even aware of their importance. Of course, we do get contradictory situations such as the Exxon *Valdez*, in which the largest company appears to have been the least prepared.

The government of Canada's Privy Council office has published a booklet entitled *Crisis Management* for the use of its many hundreds of communications officers in the field. I quote from this booklet: "Crises are inevitable. The question is not whether the federal government will find itself embroiled in a crisis, but how soon, and how big?"

Still another public relations strategy of the future is *issues management*. This is a favourite of government communicators because issues are one of the most important parts of their jobs. Issues management applies all the same principles taught in public relations textbooks, such as public opinion research to find out what the issues are and where people stand on them; content analysis of published materials to determine how the news media view the issues; clipping bureaus to identify positions taken on issues by opinion leaders and special interest groups; and analysis of issues to determine all the alternative directions in which they may flow. Issues management is based on the precept that having knowledge and having a plan increases the potential for controlling a situation.

Mass communication in the '90s will be much less "mass" than in the '80s. *Specialized media* are coming to the fore. We can now select from 40 television channels – many of which reach narrowly defined audiences. Radio targets audiences by age and interest. Unique magazines are directed to interest groups. Newspapers are made up of sections that target groups of readers (i.e., automotive, computer, lifestyles).

Industry associations will have a major part to play in communication in the 1990s. Ian Smyth, president of the Canadian Petroleum Association, says one of his main initiatives is to encourage his oil company members to shape the future, rather than react to events. Public relations programs of industry associations will be strengthened in two directions. First, to the members who will be reminded of their responsibilities and shown how to deal with them; and second, to the public, where industry associations will use honest corporate advertising and many other forms of communication to talk with the public.

The Canadian Public Relations Society embraces practitioners in the following specialized fields: investor relations; public affairs; issues management; employee communications; health care; crisis management; and opinion/attitude research.

Public relations will in future be positioned, together with lawyers, as part of the management advisory team for public responsibility.

There is an apparent void in ethics, social responsibility, and the ability to take the "long view" that exists in many organizations today, and professional public relations practitioners are uniquely suited to assume this role. It is a role necessarily at the highest management level, one which impacts directly on the bottom line in long-term business considerations, on public trust in our government institutions and on public support of our non-profit organizations. It is a role we must accept – but more, it is a role we must demand as the conscience of the organizations we serve and for the betterment of society as a whole. It is necessary in terms of ethics, in support of the "public good," and as the essential instrument of an organization's formulation of successful policy. Public relations must seize the challenge, and practitioners must make themselves heard in the boardrooms, the shop floors, and the opinion leadership of the nation.

For public relations practitioners to seize the remarkable challenge and opportunity available to them, they must speak with a strong and unified professional voice. This voice can be forged now – not an indeterminate number of years in the future – if practitioners have the will. This can be achieved by using, demanding, and selling public relations accreditation as the mark of professionalism, pushing the recruitment of all practitioners into one strong professional society, and, most critically, applying their expertise in a concentrated effort to raise the profile of that society, and to mandate the highest levels of member professionalism and continuing professional development as a requirement for membership. The time is here for public relations to assume a meaningful and leading role in society.

If public relations professionals really want to be recognized by management in the 1990s, management must hear them using the right language and understanding their problems, while at the same time relaying to them the concepts that they will not hear from their other professional advisors. I refer to concepts like public opinion research, group focus discussions, corporate advertising, exclusive interviews with influential reporters, meeting community action groups at the table and resolving differences, crisis planning, and environmental protection.

I have been in the field since 1954. This is the first time I have ever felt that I could say honestly and genuinely that public relations has come of age. The 1990s belong to people in our business.

Yes, of course, lawyers will always have a part to play. And management planners and the financial community will always be out there policing the bottom line. But the table is set for one more group in the 1990s. It is the public relations professional that is trained to look at things from both management's point of view and the public's point of view; who knows how to find out what the public is thinking and relay that message to management; and who can formulate communications programs which will increase public understanding and alter attitudes towards the organization. It is our role to guide the corporation in managing that most important financial risk of all: the risk beneath the bottom line.

CHAPTER 17

REFLECTIONS

Frequently, students and young practitioners ask for a comparison of PR careers in the three sectors I have worked in: army, public, and private. The answer requires reflection on past and present experience and contemplation about the future.

An army PR career is unique. It is more than a career; it is a way of life. In the military you wear a uniform; your status in the organization is either on your sleeves or shoulders. Your lifestyle is disciplined by tradition and training. And you must learn to take orders and carry them out before you can give orders. Before you can practise PR in the army, you must become a soldier. The training is physically and mentally demanding. It is this training that teaches you how the army operates.

If you are married or intending to marry, it is vital that your wife understands that she too will belong to the army community. That has advantages and disadvantages. One of the main causes of pressure is the husband will often be away from his family, sometimes for extended periods. Thus, the wife has more than normal responsibility for raising the children.

When I was at Carlyle Barracks in Pennyslvania, the distinguished author of *Lee's Lieutenants*, Douglas F. Freeman, was one of our visiting speakers. Many military people consider his books the definitive work on the war between the states. His subject was: "The Qualities of an Officer." He stunned his listeners by opening his address with the importance of selecting a wife who could appreciate, understand, and raise a family in the military environment. He spent more time on the topic that the students expected before turning to the qualities required of an officer.

I'm still not certain whether I selected Colleen or she me. But she became an enthusiastic member of that gallant sorority, the wives of servicemen. Despite my being frequently away from home, she successfully raised four children while we were members of the army community. We celebrated our 50th Anniversary on 6 June 1992, the 48th anniversary of the Normandy Invasion. We were together for only three anniversaries in the first 25 years. A significant advantage of this way of life is that the community immediately closes ranks and assists those who need it. I didn't worry when I was away from home.

The Chain of Command – Reporting Channels

My experience of practising PR in the army was satisfying. The PR "chain of command" was excellent. Either as a commanding officer of a PR unit or director of PR, I always had access to the commander. For routine day-to-day direction, guidance, or information, I reported to the commander's chief of staff. Also I was a member of the commander's Orders Group – the Army Council at Defence Headquarters, Ottawa (in the private sector, the Management Committee), where the deliberations provided the information I needed on the plans, policies, problems, and future activities, not only of the command but of units, for example, in Prairie Command, which incorporated the reserve and regular force army units of Saskatchewan, Manitoba, and northwestern Ontario. At these committee meetings I was expected to discuss the PR aspects of the policies, plans, and future activities.

On fast-breaking incidents I had direct access to the brigadier, but I made certain that the chief of staff was kept in the picture, if possible before seeing the brigadier. If that wasn't possible, then I would see him immediately after.

My experience with senior civil service managers was similar to the army. They were supportive and cooperative, making for a satisfying working environment. My first appointment was as an assistant director and, therefore, I reported to the director of Information Services, Mr. M. Erb. When promoted to director of PR in Energy, Mines and Resources, I reported to the deputy minister.

Today many more Information Services director generals and directors are members of department management committees and report to the deputy minister than when I was in the public service. This reporting line is essential for achieving effective PR. Organizations not employing this reporting line, public or private sector, should review the experience and competence of the director of PR. If that individual does not have the prerequisites to be a member of the management committee, then management training should be provided. Failing that, a PR officer with the necessary skills should be appointed.

On one occasion in the public service, I declined an appointment that meant a promotion because I would not have had direct access to the deputy minister.

The PR People

Initially the employment of journalists as PR practitioners became the established pattern.

In 1914 Walter Scott Thompson, news editor of the Montreal *Herald*, was appointed press representative by the Grand Trunk and Grand Pacific Trunk Railways.

Dr. Walter Herbert joined the Canadian Wheat Pool in 1924 and later was promoted and transferred to Winnipeg. His job was to warn farmers who sold their grain privately that they were breaking the law, and if necessary, he would bring charges against them. He soon found he got better results by talking to the farmers and explaining pool benefits. In the Great Depression, he opened "Business Relations Consultants Limited," the first private PR consultant firm in Canada. Two of Walter's accounts were the United Grain Growers and Western Steel Wares. He had left the practice of law to become a PR consultant. A life member of the CPRS, he was influential in advancing the cause of PR education. He was the first Chief Examiner of the CPRS accreditation program.

Education

In 1940, the two professional organizations that have contributed so much to PR and communications education were established. They are the Canadian Public Relations Society (CPRS) and the International Association of Business Communicators (IABC).

In the United States, the American Association of Industrial Editors was founded in 1938 and the International Council of Industrial Editors in 1941. The two merged in 1941 to form the International Association of Business Communicators.

In 1974, the Canadian Industrial Editors' Association joined IABC and adopted the IABC name. In Canada, IABC is administered by an eastern and a western board of directors. The IABC headquarters is in San Francisco, California.

In Canada, like the IABC, two provincial organizations were the foundation of the CPRS. They were the PR people located in Montreal and Toronto. In the 1940s, they began to recognize the need for exchanging public relations knowledge and experience. In 1948 six charter members met on 23 March 1948 to elect officers and directors of Montreal's Canadian Public Relations Society. The Montreal and Toronto groups merged and the first national president of CPRS was elected in 1953.

The two organizations have stimulated and assisted the academic community in establishing not only PR courses, but faculties of communication in Canadian universities and community colleges.

The University of Calgary offers a unique course in communications, leading to a master's degree with or without thesis. The degree with thesis requires full-time attendance for two years. The degree without thesis is provided to fully employed practitioners, the lectures being held in the evenings. These students may take more than three years to obtain their degrees.

CPRS and IABC both have programs of education and training to stimulate professional advancement, and each has developed a code of ethics and standards, required for membership.

CPRS has an accreditation program whereby members can write examinations, present a PR plan, and defend it before an accreditation panel. Members successfully completing the program are awarded the distinction of APR (Accredited Public Relations) for use after their names. While competing with each other for members, chapters of the two organizations also cooperate on projects of mutual interest.

Both organizations accept members from all three sectors. Thus, the two organizations reflect the characteristics and activities of the Canadian practitioners. In 1940, there were few female practitioners. Those employed in PR held editorial positions, but the majority were involved in administration. A gradual and dramatic change has taken place since. In 1993, women comprised almost 50 percent of the CPRS membership. The international figure for IABC is more than 60 percent.

Women are making a major contribution to PR and communications. The first woman national president of CPRS, Barbara Shefield, APR, of Toronto, served in 1990–91. The first Canadian chairperson of IABC was

Sharon Paul of Toronto, elected for the 1988–89 term. Carla Gates-Morris, APR, of Halifax, was elected as CPRS president in 1992. The national CPRS executive of five has three female members. The IABC board of directors of 25 has 12 female directors, and 19 percent of the organization's fellowships are women.

The contribution of women to the practice will continue to increase. The majority of communications and PR students in Canadian universities and community colleges are women. Graduates of universities and community colleges now make up the majority of those entering the profession. The number of former journalists are the minority.

During and for a short period after the Second World War, the number of former print and broadcast journalists, news photographers, and cameramen in armed forces PR was considerable. Today the majority in the regular force are career officers. However, most militia public affairs officers are drawn from the media or PR practitioners in the private sector.

As journalists began to retire from the regular force, lectures were instituted on "The Media and Public Relations" at staff colleges. Instruction was also given on these subjects to officers in the commands from coast-to-coast.

A few former journalists in the federal government information service were appointed by the political party in power; thus, political influence has filtered down to the director level. For example, the ISO post in Washington, D.C., has usually been filled by a senior Ottawa journalist, recruited from the press gallery. If this influence becomes too widespread, it will adversely affect morale of the ISO Group, which provides only a few foreign postings. Although the career plan and manpower guidelines recommended members of the group serve abroad, only a few have had the opportunity. External Affairs' PR function abroad is carried out by foreign service officers.

During my career in the public service, the PR function for the minister was carried out by an executive assistant, appointed by the minister. The departmental ISOs, including the director of Information Services, were appointed by the federal civil service. The executive assistant carried out the information function when politics were involved. Information Services would be called upon to do research and draft speeches and news releases. If politics were involved, the minister or the executive assistant could insert the political factors. Neither I, nor the Information Services staff, became involved in politics.

The Bilingual Policy

The bilingual policy is a highly influential factor that affects careers of senior ISOs in the federal public service and public affairs officers in the military. The Glassco Commission had recommended that at least one of the two most senior officers be bilingual. This meant the unilingual officer would be English speaking, and probably not bilingual. In most instances the bilingual officer's first language was French. Quebec produces more individuals fluent in the two official languages than other provinces with large populations. For example, bilingual individuals in the Western provinces are a small percentage of the population. The bilingual policy truncated unilingual information officers' careers. It also hurt some bilingual officers whose first language was French and whose advancement was accelerated.

When the policy was introduced a "grandfather's" clause was included which exempted older ISOs, like myself, from the necessity of acquiring French. Despite this, I requested approval to attend a French training centre in Hull, Quebec, believing it would set an example for my staff. Disaster followed.

On reporting, the students were briefed on the course and told that from the next day on we were to speak to the instructors only in French. We also were told that audio tapes were available for those having recorders. These could be used at home to accelerate the learning process. I had a recorder and obtained the tapes.

For about two weeks I attended class, worked in the language laboratory and with the tapes in the evening. But it was evident I was falling behind my classmates. The tapes were frustrating me. I could not relate them to what I was being taught during the day. It was comparable to being imprisoned in a room with no doors or windows. After two weeks I went to one of our two instructors, insisted on speaking English and told him my problem. He was sympathetic. "Give me the tapes and see me after class," he said in English.

They had given me the wrong tapes. The tapes I had bore no relation to what I was being taught.

At the conclusion of the course I continued my efforts with a tutor and acquired a limited facility before I left the service. Since moving to Calgary in 1973 I've lost most of the conversational ability, but I can follow a hockey game commentary and read a limited portion of a newspaper.

To achieve senior positions in the Information Services Group and the military, it is essential to be bilingual.

Access to Information

Eight years after I left the public service, an event of great significance took place 16 July 1981. Cabinet, for the first time, provided a series of principles "to guide future development of government policies, and also to guide the public service in their communications activities." It was the first set of guidelines that applied to all departments. The principles established in these guidelines were as follows:

1. Canadians have the right to full, accurate and timely information, in compliance with the Official Languages Act, about their government so that they can exercise their rights of citizenship and take part in the democratic process fully, responsibly and in an informed manner.

2. Canadians have a right to access to government records, with exceptions, to be legally defined and ultimately interpreted by the courts, designed to protect essential public and private interests.

3. Government has the responsibility to provide the public with full, accurate and timely information about the policies, programs and legislation approved by Parliament; it also has the responsibility to inform the public of factual content of its policy proposals and of facts as it is aware of them regarding the public issues addressed by its policies.

4. Government has a corresponding responsibility to make every reasonable effort to learn of the concerns and views of Canadians, with particular attention to differences of views in different regions of the country, so as better to inform itself in establishing priorities, in developing policies, and in implementing programs which serve the interests of Canada.

5. Effective communications between citizens and government imply a reasonable effort on the part of citizens to seek the information they require to exercise

their rights of citizenship, and an obligation on the
part of government to make every reasonable effort
to provide access to information on an equal basis in
all regions of Canada.

It was the first comprehensive guidance given to the Information
Services, the media, and the public. It has had a positive effect on the provision of public information. Periodically, newspaper stories and editorials
state the information was obtained "under the legislation governing
access." Individuals of the public also have obtained information previously denied them. Guideline No. 2 is justified, as the courts provide a neutral authority capable of determining whether or not the public interest
would be damaged by release of certain information.

There are similarities between PR careers in the military and public
sectors. Loyalty is common to both. Both sectors contribute to the
achievement of Canadian objectives. Officers of the military and departments of Immigration, External Affairs, and Trade and Commerce serve a
portion of their careers in foreign countries. The experience expands their
views and appreciation of Canada, its culture, and its people.

However, there are some information problems. The army structure is
such that locating information is relatively simple, as there are no difficulties in knowing who is responsible for what. The federal government
departments are much more complex. It takes considerable time for the
new federal civil servant to become familiar with sources of information,
and it is even more difficult for the general public.

Improvements, no doubt, have been made since I left the service.
When with the Department of Energy, Mines and Resources, I contributed, in a small way, to alleviating the problems. When members of
the Information Services received a telephone request to which they did
not know the answer and were not certain where that answer could be
obtained, they took the name, address, and phone number of the caller,
then found both the source of the required information and provided it to
the caller. This avoided the possibility of callers being passed from branch
to branch or department to department, arousing the righteous wrath of
the caller.

To work successfully in federal PR it is essential to understand the system, particularly that of finance. Unless this is achieved, serious frustration will result. Quite properly, expenditure of public funds by the
Information Services are carefully scrutinized and, depending upon the
size of the expenditure, several approvals are needed.

Specific goods and services each have expenditure ceilings. If as a director you wished to exceed a ceiling, the request to do so, accompanied by the justification, is sent to the immediate superior *before* the purchase is made. In the case of contracts, a completed *pro forma* is sent to the department's finance office. The financial officer must confirm that you have sufficient funds for that particular item. If not, the questioning begins. The procedures take time, but they are necessary for the protection of the public purse.

On one occasion, my PR budget was unexpectedly and significantly reduced. The reduction was the public relations services' contribution to a new Canadian immigration office in Paris. This type of incident is not uncommon. Also, staffing a position on the public sector takes longer than in the private sector. In the public sector, procedure is all-important. In the private sector, process is less important; the credo is "get the job done quickly, effectively and economically."

The Private Sector

My experience in the private sector has been acquired solely with a public relations and advertising consultants agency. My knowledge of non-profit PR organizations and corporate PR has been acquired by observation, conversation, and reading. Non-profit organization serving a nation or community is cause driven in the interests of the nation, the community, and the people. The media has the same cause and, hence, readily assists the PR functions of non-profit organizations. This does not mean that such organizations have no PR problems, nor does it mean the media will not attack them. If substantiated, maladministration will bring down the wrath of the media. And rightly so because the non-profit organizations receive their funds from the public or from governments. Some of the issues can be complex and highly emotional (i.e., the United Way, birth control, abortion).

As in the public and military sectors, corporate communications are a staff function contributing to the achievement of operational goals. PR is not an end in itself. In the corporation, success of the function depends upon the position the function is given, its reporting lines, the skills of the PR director and staff in PR, and the director's managerial skills. Just as important are the chief executive officer's (CEOs) and line staff's knowledge of PR. The reporting lines for the PR director must provide access to the CEO when needed and to all senior executives and department heads.

To be effective, the PR director must be a member of the management committee. While PR does not generate revenue, the function must be integrated with line management.

Agencies

A PR agency is a business and the work is complex. It generates revenue by performing the PR function. It spends other peoples' (clients) money. And it must do so wisely and effectively or the client will lose money and the agency will lose the client.

In a corporation, the PR director prepares an annual budget. In an agency, a projected budget is prepared not only for the agency, but also for the work that will be done for each client. Each client rightly feels that the work given is the agency's most important work. This produces pressure that mounts as the client list increases. The staff of a PR agency must acquire business skills to add to their PR skills and knowledge. They must have presentation abilities, produce contact reports, and deal with a multitude of suppliers. Agencies recruit experienced PR people from the private and public sectors. When a position is open, they hire students who have shown a high degree of talent while serving a practicum.

PR messages of a corporation change. An agency deals with a variety of messages that are dictated by the number of clients served. The pace in an agency is fast and the margin for error is small. The staff turnover is more frequent in the agency than in the public sector or corporations.

An attractive aspect of agency work is the variety: variety of clients to be served, variety of problems to be solved, variety of businesses to be learned, and variety of skills to be acquired.

Two subjects for which agencies plan and provide instruction are crisis management (described in chapter 16) and media relations training for corporate executives. The latter takes the form of seminars, the objective of which is to sharpen executives' communication skills through news conferences and radio and television interviews. The result of this training was evident during the Oka incident in 1990. Army officers at Oka willingly provided candid interviews for print and television reporters, despite the pressure and tension they were experiencing.

More recently, the media and the Canadian public recognized these skills when more senior officers, also under stress, were interviewed on the subject of peacekeeping versus peacemaking. The most prominent examples are the interviews given in Ottawa by the chief of staff of the armed forces, General A.J. de Chastelain, who was appointed Canada's ambassador to the United States in January 1993, and by General Lewis Mackenzie, while serving in Sarajevo in 1992.

Corporate CEOs who feel insecure about dealing with reporters and, as a result, do not act as spokespersons for their organizations, are right to appoint a member of their staff who has the required skills and knowledge. However, these skills can be acquired, and the CEO who acquires them will project greater authority, inspire greater trust, and maintain sound media relations.

Technology

The private sector created the technology that has impacted heavily on all three sectors. Television, satellites, telefacsimile machines, cellular telephones, and computers have revolutionized communications and research. Retyping entire letters and manuscripts because of errors disappeared with the arrival of the word processor. This resulted in clerical staff reductions.

The creation of data bases put research at practitioners' fingertips. Two major Canadian data bases are Info Globe and Infomart. Info Globe provides information from the *Globe and Mail* newspaper going back to 1977. Infomart provides information from more than 80 data bases, including media outlets, *Maclean's* magazine, product and trademark information, as well as eight wire services.

Full text content from the media in Canada and the United States is now available electronically. Canadian and U.S. practitioners can access information in both countries.

With the North American Free Trade Agreement between Canada, the United States, and Mexico to come on line, the importance of data bases will be even greater. Information on trends, competitors' activities, and background for use in presentation to prospective clients are a few of the subjects affected.

Data base companies charge membership fees and for time on-line. Cost can be controlled by having a staff member trained in accessing information. Random search by inexperienced staff is costly.

A study in the United States concluded that research and collection of background information from electronic databases reduced manual procedures time by as much as 64 percent.

Television

The communications revolution created by television has intensified media competition. Television not only has the advantage of greater speed of news delivery than print, it can present the event live. This creates problems for the print media, but also politicians, their governments, and the military. This reality surfaced during the 1991 Gulf War.

During the build-up phase, television networks presented newscasts of interviews with authorities in the capitals of coalition countries, Iraq, and neutral nations.

During the initial stages of a war-threatening crisis, competent reporting by journalists and responses by politicians are vital factors in the battle of words that lead to peace or war. Television's speed severely reduces the time for checking facts and formulating dispatches and responses. The burden of responsibility borne by journalists and politicians in such a crisis is tremendous.

Saddam Hussein used the bombing of a Baghdad bunker that coalition forces had believed to be a communications centre to his advantage. Television news teams were brought to the bunker to film the dead and the devastation. The image created was one of indiscriminate bombing of civilians.

Journalists and the military agree that reporting of the Gulf War left much to be desired. Veteran Canadian war correspondents concur. Inaccurate reports of Iraqi missile attacks on Israel came close to bringing Israel into the war.

Saddam Hussein used television to split the coalition alliance before the outbreak of fighting. While he did not succeed, he did create concern among authorities in the coalition capitals about the impact on their populations and those of the neutral countries. Hussein, however, erred seriously when he appeared on television with foreign hostages and their children. He enraged the coalition countries' publics and damaged his image in the neutral countries.

Brian Stewart, CBC war correspondent in the Gulf War and a member of the Canadian War Correspondents' Association, made an interesting point about the Gulf War: "This was the first war in the history of humanity where the representative of the other belligerent appeared almost nightly in the homes of the world."

Little was transmitted during the conflict of combat between the opposing ground forces. What the public saw were coalition aircraft equipped with "smart bombs," and guided missiles attacking communications centres, anti-aircraft guns, missile sites, and bridges. Technologically, it is possible to transmit live action of ground forces in combat; but should it be done? The media industry, the government, and the military must formulate the answer in peacetime. Because of the need for security, military PR has some special and important problems of its own created by technology. Their solution truly is a matter of life and death.

The Future

Major changes in the PR function are just over the horizon. The most dramatic changes are the means of processing, storing, and distributing information.

However, the most important change for those in PR will be a slow but steady one. The demand for higher and higher degrees of professionalism will increase. This will manifest itself in Cabinet ministers' offices, where politically appointed executive assistants may well be individuals who have acquired a master's or doctorate degree in communication. This phenomena is developing in the private sector. Extended academic training will provide executives highly skilled in research, communication ethics, and the theory and practice of PR. Thus, the limited time available to ministers of the crown and corporate executives to discuss PR problems and solutions will be put to better use and the results will be more effective.

Whatever the future there will be one constant aspect – the scrutiny of PR in the private and public sectors by government opposition, the media, and the public. To date, modern PR has stood up under that scrutiny and should continue to do so.

Ethics

The success of PR officers is dependent upon ethics and efficiency in working with others, especially the media. The public's judgements are made on information disseminated by the three sectors. For the judgements to be sound, the information must be based on facts – fair and unbiased. Highly debatable propositions must be identified as such. The public must not be deceived into believing such propositions are facts.

One principle of conduct in the CPRS Code of Professional Standards states:

> A member shall adhere to the highest standards of honesty and shall not knowingly disseminate false or misleading information.

Failure to observe that credo is counterproductive. The media renders a vital national service through constant scrutiny of information services output.

Reflecting on 50 years in the field has erased any lingering regret at being deprived of a medical career. Public relations has enabled me to work with and learn from many talented people, to come to a greater appreciation of Canada by serving outside its borders, to contribute to the development of young practitioners, to participate in peacekeeping, to learn about the medical profession through client hospitals, and to witness federal government activities up close.

Because it has been so engrossing, Colleen and I are determined to retain our semi-retirement status, and we hope we will be permitted to witness and participate in the continuing changes that will occur as a united Canada enters a new century.